MATTHEW MEAD

THE AUTUMN–BORN IN AUTUMN

By Matthew Mead

POETRY

Identities
The Administration of Things
The Midday Muse
A Sestina at the End of Socialism
Walking Out of the World

TRANSLATIONS
(*with Ruth Mead*)

WOLFGANG BÄCHLER: Doors of Smoke
HORST BIENEK
(Unicorn German Series)
ELISABETH BORCHERS
(Unicorn German Series)
JOHANNES BOBROWSKI: Shadow Lands
GÜNTER BRUNO FUCHS: The Raven
CHRISTIAN GEISSLER: songs from the old folk's home
MAX HÖLZER: Amfortiade
URS OBERLIN: Flamingo Dance
CHRISTA REINIG: The Tightrope Walker
HEINZ WINFRIED SABAIS: The People and the Stones

Word for Word
Selected Translations from German Poets

Matthew Mead

The Autumn-Born in Autumn

SELECTED POEMS

ANVIL PRESS POETRY

Published in 2008
by Anvil Press Poetry Ltd
Neptune House 70 Royal Hill London SE10 8RF
www.anvilpresspoetry.com

This book is published with financial assistance
from Arts Council England

Designed and set in Monotype Bembo by Anvil
Printed and bound in Great Britain
by Hobbs the Printers Ltd

ISBN 978 85646 400 3

A catalogue record for this book
is available from the British Library

The author's moral rights have been asserted in accordance
with the Copyright, Designs and Patents Act 1988

An earlier version of 'The Poetry of Matthew Mead'
by Dick Davis appeared in *PN Review 42*, 1984

for Ruth

Introduction

These poems are taken from *Identities and other poems* (1967), *The Administration of Things* (1970), *The Midday Muse* (1979), *A Sestina at the End of Socialism* (1998) and *Walking Out of the World* (2004).

I have to thank Malcolm Rutherford and Peter Jay for help in making this selection. Jobs for the Boys. And for me a brief haunting and the conclusion that when one has written one's poems there is nothing more to say.

M. M.

Contents

The Midday Muse (1979)

A Sestina at the End of Socialism (1996)

Walking Out of the World (2004)

Identities

But the man that is will shadow
The man that pretends to be.

T.S.ELIOT

It turned out later that he was
a fourteen-year-old Mexican
armed with a water-pistol.

RAYMOND CHANDLER

I

After Passchendaele
After Katyn
After Auschwitz
After Kronstadt
We stand here

After Asquith
After Beria
After Noske
We stand here

What footfall?
What valley what field what forest
What streets in the morning sun
After the streets of Nagasaki?
Mask, persona,
Alias, pseudonym;
We stand here.

Why should we flee, Jahveh?
    Where are the lightnings,
    The scorched prophets?
'In millions of hearts

'burns the inextinguishable
'flame of his word.'.
Apollo: carven flame.
Christ by candlelight.

And that he mount the unbuilt steps
To the unraised altar
                    with sky for roof
                    and star for pinnacle
                    sumus in fide

We stand here.
We stand in the press.
We stand here alone.

II

Will you remember me Tatania
When your map of this country is folded,
When you see no more the low tower and the hills,
The humped bridge, the stream through the osier-holt?

We pause at the kissing-gate,
The spinney twists into evening;
The wind travels far Tatania
And you must follow.
When 'September' and 'remember' rhyme
Shall I rhyme them for a café translation?

The hills wait as always for the caressing eye,
The eager feet of glory or the warning beacon;
Over successive fields, breakers of hedge
Lift to a legacy of skyline:
Will you remember me Tatania
As I cling to these landmarks and scars
Which fade from your mind?

We stand here in the last of day,
The hills wait
The fields are a green sea.
And nearer the light fails
Changes and fades and our eyes
Clutch line of branch
Silhouette of leaf . . .

When Lazarus lies in his long tomb and dead leaves
Tremble in their forgetting dance,
Will you remember me Tatania?
Shall I come like a ghost to trouble joy?
Tatania, Tatania, what will you remember?
Here, with your lips on mine,
Who do you say I am?

III

How narrowly he eyes his sun,
My lamp. And shuffles to the chair
Through trackless wastes of my fine turkey carpet.
Do Bedouin squat and long for shade?
He licks his lips, the mirage left in the cell.

How helplessly his hands clasp
One another; unclip, clench,
Fall palm-down on his knees.
No hand shall reach to bear him up
But mine, fingering the stony dossier.

Paved roads, polished leather, avenues;
Spurred heel, meadowland, the great plain;
Silent they move in the forest; wrapped foot,
Bare foot, claw in the slime;
A wind screams round the naked rock.
He is the rock. The rock will break.

IV

We stand here.
Statisti.

My pills are good pills
rustle and chink
container and carton and can
all cars are good cars
but our cars are *sacred*
the next scream you hear will be MAN.

'there is no such THING
         as saturation point'

My pills are good pills
interim interim
dreams you can drive in your sleep
hand washes hand
our after-death service
washes bone-white and bone-deep.

'for Christ's sake, Stan,
         TRY and be a merchant'

Buy it today
that agglutinous yellow
matches the STYLE of your heart
our workers sweat
at contented machine tools
producing the part of a part.

'buy him and THEN he'll buy you'

Mixed in a minute
served in a second
slashes the stomach for days

interim interim
listprice and discount
traders must follow the phrase.

'for all practical purposes
            YOU ARE the product'

My pills are good pills
my self's a good self
complete with a soul to consume
last thing at night
AND BANISH THE IMAGES
don't just say 'Dreadful' say 'Doom'.

We stand here
for all practical purposes
for christ's sake or near offer.
At our heels a question-mark
        in our heads the moon.

V

Am I not also a candidate for fame
   to be heard in song
With blossom in my long
   hair and a sweet name
   to be known by at the whorled ear?
I have heard the roar
   in the sea-shell
   and stood mid-water
I have seen one bud swell
   and woken mid-forest
   to keep a green tryst.

Am I not also bound by the boom
   of oaths to love for long
Delay one overlong
   to call me? Whom
   I have seen linger
(it was here)
   by the white wall
   of breaking water
And smile
   as I walked, her truest
   ghost,

And sang and signed my name
   on air. I sing
To be in her song-
   ster-plume
   one feather
Plucked. Am I not another
   candidate to call?
   I walk here
And sing, year-fall, world-fall,
   till the call ring clearest
   in which I trust.

VI

Length and breadth of the head
length of the little finger
length of the outstretched arms
from middle to middle finger end;
the porter cannot be sure
the deskclerk does not remember;
and Graebe:
'I well remember the girl
'slim and with black hair,
'who, as she passed me,
'pointed to herself and said:
'"Twenty-three years old"'
and naked, entered the death-pit.
The convolutions of that ear
may not be repeated in history
and if man is the measure of all things
to what assizement shall we come?

Length and breadth of the right ear
length from the elbow
to the end of the middle finger;
each is unique in dimension.
Nevertheless after fifty faces
on the same street, after fifty noses
and a hundred eyes . . .
People, Proletariat, Volk –
an anthropometric norm.
Height, length of the trunk
length of the left foot.
The one promise worth making:
    Immortality.

To resume from this dust the loved flesh
as from scorched clay the monsoon rains
wrench a brief tribute of green . . .
it is impossible; or that one should walk
from the grave telling of what may be;
or that essence be leached from these ashes . . .

An everest of skulls.
An oxford street of tibiae.
If these are the bones of my grandfather
Where is his beard and short temper?
Does he plough the field of heaven
And harvest the golden floor?

Where are the useful, clanking spectres?
Where are the ladies in brocaded gowns
Whose touch was the dawn wind?
He came at dawn in the clean air
In the clear light and our eyes
Fumbled at his face like blind men's fingers.
Length of the outstretched arms
From middle to middle finger end.
Skin-food, 'indelible' kisses, mascara.
Body: metaphor for death.

VII

My verses, Ochkasty, and your music,
Your mathematical progression
To the door of Terpsichore's boudoir,
These brought us a summons to dine
At the groaning table of Paren,
To wolf his steak, to guzzle his wine,
To play 'feet' with his wife (beneath table)
To ogle his sister.

The hordes of the East are unfed.
I felt them, Ochkasty,
Their hunger a wolf-pack,
Round the broken meats of that board.
Wolf-faces, wolf-bellies,
Landless, arms like sticks.
Most terrible were the eyes of the children,
Heirs to famine; Romulus, Remus unsuckled.

You would share your bread with them and perish,
Remembered by 'Tone Poem: Hunger'.
I am 'aware of the problem'.
See, it clutters a poem.

I weigh our undoubted genius
Against the million-death headline.
I spoon up my onion soup
And know that I am not God.

The hordes of the East are unfed.
If Io herself has failed them
          let us despatch
With teats and feeding bottles
               Paren to lands of morning.

He serves a very good dinner.

He may meet cannibals.

VIII

I am Morold
already slain

I am a boy
who sings mast high
of another love

I am Melot
the betrayer
to be slain
by Kurvenal

I am Kurvenal

I am Mark
king of a clear grief
and a reasoned mourning.

How then shall I drink
and lie beside you in life
and lie with you in death?

Or are we singing some other opera?

IX

Gentlemen of the Geheime Staatspolizei (retired)
and men of other secret police organisations

AND

        that shower of ex-muzhiks
        over there STOP FIDDLING
        with the initials on your epaulettes

           (sings)   you'll always be
                    the gay pay oo
                    to me

STAND STILL

Now chaps

assuming that his testicles have been crushed,
   his finger nails torn out, his teeth smashed in,
   his nose broken

assuming that he has stood an arms-length from
   the wall for long enough, that he has sat
   on the broken chair for twenty-four hours,
   that he is blind with light, that he must
   urinate every twenty minutes

assuming that the suitable degree of emaciation,
   weakness and subjection has been attained

   that he cannot remember sleep
   that he desires only sleep

SEROV! STOP TALKING . . .

Now lads

if you have seen the ills of our time,
the disease, its course,
its deviations

Lads

is there anything which a good burst
from a sub-machine-gun wouldn't cure?

X

Marsiglio questions, Hus burns;
Flacius and Melanchthon
                 dispute in vain
What the little brown monk really meant;
What is there but loot, von Hutten,
   in riding against the Archbishop?

'Ecrasez l'infame!' Gaols,
Jesuits and salons. Lisbon
                 topples: Pombal.
All matters conclude in blood;
What is there but profit, St. Just,
   in cutting the head off a king?

And also in Trier, Marx –
Like a Talmudic spectre
                 haunting Lenin.
'If you must die what are you dying for?'
What is there but satisfaction, Kinto,
   as the ice-pick splits the skull?

XI

'You must meet Julie, oolala'
– and then his hands describe in air
  a form most likely to recur
  with grace this side the last hurrah.

'You must meet Julie, oolala'
– such clicking of the teeth and tongue
  ought properly to lead a young
  Propertius to Cynthia.

Joan sleeps a little earth away,
Lucinda has three sons, a daughter.
Feeling for what was felt before
My hands rehearse their yesterday.

'You must meet Julie'. And I must.
Julie forgive me each faux-pas.
I must meet Julie. Oolala.
So many other girls are dust.

XII

The leopard-men
    sang the song
    of the leopard-clan:
    'claw . . . . . .
    '. . . . . lithe . . . . .
    'soft, soft, our swiftness'
And killed in the leopard-name –
the Great Cat over the Moon.

And that was by night.

So that the day – where they walked as men,
Blunt-fingered, with only a little hair –
Held no ferocity to strike at trivia.
The day was to be lived. Not for the sake
Of night. But for itself. Other than that . . .
Soft, soft, the shadow moved at heel.

We can fill up the hours with small songs,
Regretting a bright head or a brief beauty
Gone like a night-quenched flame . . .

            'I was seen going down a hill
                    by Edward Arlington Robinson'

There are open streets to maintain by order
Until chaos comes. There is a space
In which to walk as men.
                    To be missed at noon,
The laid table and the expected hour.
Identity is a problem for pretenders.

Star on the night-blue cloth
                    of heaven
Star-son at the pause of labour

(the birth enrolled for death
in the pause of piebald day)

Unless he can, wreath piled on wreath,
  Sustain each honour;
Unless he can, plain title and clear proof,
  Speak truly, word and echo;
Each name is grey with breath
                    – an alias forgotten.

XIII

Not with the gift of frost, fire-delicate on the pane
  – Leaf, stem and flower transcribed:

   'See here the fingers,
     All summer and spring remembered,
     Here set in white, diamond on glass,
     Crystal built in tints of white,
     Here the budding, here the full leaf . . .'

Not with that gift; stiffly his fingers trace
Through sham and sweat
    a still-life without reflection;
Or lose touch as memory shifts, corrupt,
Through the half-thaw of noon
    in lukewarm meditation;
Or an opaque pattern
       of transparency
       melts under the hand.

And cold is the element; his fate
To move where nothing stirs
But shiver and apprehension,
To speak with imprecision
      of elusive colour;
He comes cold through many summers
To sign 'Anon'.
       Under a fur hood
Indifferent eyes, clouded breath:
   'Unless the words dance
     you have done nothing'.

Tongue-tip and finger-tip touch silence, zero.
Filigree leaf and star must draw the light
  To their design,

Dead rhythms of darkness
   Dance through halls of flame.
Night must sing in the dawn crystal
   And when the pane is blind with light

   All this must be set down.

from 'Render unto Ezra'

II

If we have homes
    he has instructed the architect

If there are other lands
    he has charted the roads
    and sea-routes

Lost ages are the early wind
              and the feel of it.

Chloris Periplum

The hymn is sung, the lesson read,
And all our sins shall be forgiven.
Chloris, I see you bow your head;
Christ hesitates, and clings to heaven.

Fidelity

Landor, I cannot think it fair!
My song is sweet, my words are true,
And you are dust that does not dare;
And Rose is faithful still to you.

Translator to Translated

I.M. Johannes Bobrowski

River, plain,
tree, the bird
in flight, habitation
and name, strange
to me, never strange
to you – the child's
eye, the soldier's
step, the known
threshold.

I crossed the plain
slowly, saw your fire
in the distance.
Have I set the tree
askew on your sky,
does your bird hover
strangely?
Love
translates
as love.
Her song sung
in a strange land.

An air that kills.

A Poem in Nine Parts

One: *A throat constricted in Cherrytree Road*

Skirts, head-scarves, skin-tight slacks,
Lips of blood, breasts by e.e. cummings,
Girls hurry up the hill against the wind
To work at the sweet-factory;
It is true that two women
(Furtseva and Pauker?)
Trudge middle-age
Like a theory of increasing misery,
Yet nyloned, sandalled, stiletto-heeled,
Girls hurry up the hill
To hive as worker-queens,
Climbing to an eight a.m. start
With the jounce of a gay proletariat
In a confection of spring sunshine.

This proletariat hurrying up the hill
Is gayer, at a guess, George,
Than any proletariat you have seen.

Hey yeeorgi, Georgi Karpov!
Does the committee still meet Wednesdays
To smash the occasional ikon?

Are all forms gingerbread or icing-sugar
To be munched or melted
Or crumbled into crumbs?

George boy, are things really under control,
Jung untranslated, the patriarch lap-dog still,
The peasants safe in aseptic agro-towns?

Hey yeeorgi, expert in liturgy,
What form of word endures?
Beware George of the whispered response,
Beware of the metaphysics of
          'any other business'.

Head-scarf, mouse-hair, red-head, flame,
Blonde, ash-blonde, suicide-blonde,
The heads bob up the hill
In a highlight of spring sunshine.
Theorist! be subtle
As the shades of Inecto.
Mummd, tampaxt, lyrild, girls
Girded by playtex and twilfit, girls
Hurry up the hill like living dolls.
Today, the consumer market.
Tomorrow, the world.

Lady, your absence is proper,
This hill, I know, is not Helicon.
Forgive me, if having seen men, I pray:
   'Teach women how to prevail'
And then wince at the women.
I have watched with the eyes of a dead man
Who has praised the living
Which were yet alive
And come upon cardboard silhouettes
In the eight a.m. of nothing.

Two: *A bearing taken on Beechwood Rise*

Under the ice-cliffs in the winter noon
following round-cape, glacier edge and inlet,
delineating islet, cliff and talus,
coming on sea-ice clear of jutting glacier,
facing a sudden north, a frozen sea . . .

Plodding across an Anglo-Saxon hell,
the frosty fog like lamp-black on the lung,
an east wind probing for the lumbar nerve,
knowing no ghost by name, no soul by sight,
despising most the accent of the damned . . .

Sitting in draughts, catching the common cold,
crouching upon a claustrophobic hearth,
coughing again, spreading the common cold,
sniffing thick-headed up a chilly stair
to harrow icy bedrooms . . .

Lady, I was content in the cold,
It was enough
To feel the first flakes
Melt in my face
And to lie alone in the long cold;
The frost sufficed and truly
I have forgotten such songs
As gentle the air with your name
And might alter your cold eyes.
I would be silent now,
Walk to my long home,
Sign 'Anon' and sleep

But across gardens, pavements, graves,
A punctilious season moves
Lighting the blossomed tree

And your daughters climb a hill
To become puppets of time and motion
And spoil for a works engineer.

The earth smiles like a girl, assured of her attraction,
Impatient feet stamp the worn stone.
Even I, in cold blood, come to the meeting place.

Three: *A confusion at Epiphany*

Where is the winter queen?
This maiden (no maiden)
Couches on straw. Animal pungencies
Sidle upon the air about creation.

The animal creates the animal,
Corrupts the myth and disconcerts the star.
Where is the Winter queen?

These eyes grow large and soft
Not scorning now the stable
And the floor of beaten earth.

Night loses mystery, we see no star.
Where is the brow of snow, the gaze of ice
Holding us in the season which we know?
Where is the winter queen, without compassion?

Four: *Aide-memoir for an archetype of the Dark Mechanic*

carpark officeblock and drive
timeclock yard and railway siding
puddle duckboard rusty castings
gantry on a greasy sky
chimney spout of smoke machine shop
finished plant repair shop plate shop
hammers ring too loud for words.

angle channel sheet and bar
bender guillotine and rolls
forge and burner welder's arc
grinder's comet-tail of spark
foreman office timeclerk jobcard
steward bonus time allowed
hammers ring too loud for words.

jig and tool design and template
cut machine and countersink
centre-lathe and pile of turnings
skim-milk stream of cutting oil
sudden in a greasy silence
teabreak centreforward bonus
rate for job and one off batch.

rust and scale and waiting card
shotblast grit red oxide primer
chargehand holes are out of line
steward strike dispute redundant
productivity convenor
slump and scar and compensation
officeskirt and ringing hammers.

russia management mismanage
walk on concrete work in metal
concrete and metallic world
flesh of wife and fear for children
russia crèche and revolution
rights class job redundant hunger
hammers ring too loud for words.

Five: *Several ways of ignoring the end a revolution*

Trumpet again the triumph of Soviet steel
Bring back the springing flesh of ballerinas
That the spectre of communism be seen
                only in the public rooms.

⋆

There is no action but the blind rebellion,
The fingers, closing on a throat,
Seen suddenly as hairy, not our own;
And then our own. And ours the rage
Masking amazement at the broken face
Swaying before us as we strike again.

There is no meaning but the tropic blood,
There is no order but the breaking wave,
No truth but deafness to danger –
The command unheard before the guns speak.

⋆

Objectively he is a White Guard
Riding across Red Square
To convert the tomb of Lenin
Into a comfort station.

⋆

When in this monolithic state
I find your dress above your knees
Chloris my rising shall equate
Your needs to your abilities.

⋆

The doctors are plotting
An adolescent disorder.

★

I have stood in a shouldered square with an elbow raking
    my ribs
While the metaphor of a slow and heavy beast brooded
    above the crowd;
I have smelt a shuttered room
Under an open sky.
I have seen the traitor bow
(lick-spittle and alone)
And heard my traitor self
Cheer a proposal to delete compassion.

The great beast, groomed and passive,
Is tethered among ephemeral junk.
My life is a shrunken space,
A furtive shrug before the stupid guards
And clever judges of my acquiescence.

'We have become beggars
'We have been oppressed
'We are breathless . . .'
These words will sigh again
Across a stinking square;
And the metaphor charge waist-high.

★

The moon withers in state.

Six: *A draft for the shop-steward*

The ice-men sit where the snow-maiden sat;
They do not understand the cold.

We do not ask for gentler blizzards,
More level drifts of snow, nor that winds
Shall cut us less keenly. We are not negotiating
For mornings without misery nor for afternoons
Lighter at four o'clock.
Thaws at midnight are no part of our demand,
Our argument contains no tropical images.
We want the rate for a condition of cold.

The ice-men sit where the snow-maiden sat,
They talk of furnaces, heating values, insulation;
They would wrap us all in electric blankets.

Into the long cold issues

        a failure to agree.

Seven: *A dream and a doctrine*

In her first sleep
She stood alone in a high place
Under a crescent of cold light
She stood alone as in a place prepared;
Below a bare summit
Black branches lifted
In withered acclamation.

In the dark dress of night
A girl in a high place
Looked down upon a valley
Churned and torn and silvered
Nomansland;
And knew the landscape as earth,
Earth given to moonscape,
Earth after man, a female desolation,
Earth before star and snake.

She felt herself fade,
Her flesh seek out her phantom;
Sleep was a fluttering curtain
                                    torn aside
And night worn threadbare.

Because she does not come
        the girls go up the hill
        keeping the short state
        of blossom-festivals;
Eternity is her measure
        the sun her seamstress.

Because she does nothing
        the girls go up the hill
        against the wind

into clock-numbered captivity;
She is mistress of the winds
     which serve in freedom.

Because she is silent
     the girls go up the hill
     their sweet flesh, dumb for years,
     crying an hour in exultation;
Her truth is this cry
     shaped to a clear speech.

Therefore, as is well known,
     the girls go up the hill
     and the wind presses on them
     a form of archaic rumour
In which, at her behest,
     the words make sense and song.

Whisper it in the boudoirs of Vitimsk,
Tell it – the hair-driers whine –
In the beauty salons of Shumaisa;
Word for the laundrettes of Harlesden
For the powder rooms of Konitsa
Or wherever, across garden fences,
Runs, barbed, the oral tradition;
Hear O ye cities
And discussion circles at Chofa:

     'Because she does nothing
          she is nothing'.

She dreams.
She has dreamt you.
It is enough.

Eight: *To a poet a thousand years hence*

Mine is a voice for quiet rooms,
I think that you may not hear it;
A managerial Apollo does not hear it
And it is unadvised by me
That Mercury recommends dividends
Which do not comfort Pluto.
Councils of state, ceremonies of death and birth,
Strike meetings, learned assemblies
– at all these am I silent,
    absent and silent, not a slurred
    vowel, not a bitten consonant.
Mine is a voice for quiet rooms
Where, to the manner born,
A girl may ignore the drone of my small heart.

And you have bathed and come with full belly
To warmth and suave light
And to this English text?
Lenin and Stenka Razin
Simbursk bleibt Simbursk
The night breathless
                with nightingales
The orchards white with blossom . . .
Or a circle of hungry dark
Squats in the woodfire's flicker?
The machine tool has damaged the psyche;
Stalin, O sunken sun . . .
Honours fall thick upon me
    as wreaths on the brow of Bukharin.
We meet, if we meet, my friend
In a wilderness of yellow pages.
A thousand years is as long as death.

Mine is a voice for quiet rooms.
I sit in rooms thick with music
I counterfeit silence
And set this word on the evening wind:
She is the snowfield, the blossom,
The song you sing. Like a deliberate archaism
I think that I bring you no news.

Nine: *A six o'clock shadow*

The first dusk drifts
through the lights of the shopping centre
veiling the girls who wait,
their reflections poised in plate-glass,
for the heavy date.

The first dusk drifts
by appointment to counsel love
that enchantments are what they seem.
The one tree in the street is heavy
with ornamental blossom.

rockabye baby
the world goes by
to nightfall and neontime
rockabye baby
the world goes by
wait in the doorway
and see if he comes
and if he knows why
the first dusk drifts
and his banner over you
is ornamental blossom.

The first dusk drifts;
gaze in a darkening glass,
you are not made fair in vain;
you are made fair that blood
rise to the call of trumpets
beat with the wild drum
that singing break forth
at agate windows
that pleasant borders

be rich with song
that midnight lie weightless
sharing breath and meaning.

The moon renews her light.
The song made new on lips
that never sang before
(as in Verona, here)
sings of the first and highest
Mother of mothers,
fathered without fault;
here as in Delos
her sure sign crowns the night
as the moon renews her light.

We sing beneath no green tree
and beside no speaking stream
but amid the steel, glass,
concrete of conurbation,
yet though we play by ear
we have the song by heart;
hear us, mistress,
hear us in this city
and hear us
whether these black stones
    stand or fall;
we sing at one with all
    which cries to be born.

Lady, 'young-as-ever', thrice-potent
to cause, to measure, to fulfil,
for this night are we false to our day
    and 'our age' cracks.
Mistress of fortune
    preserve our fortune,

Ruler of darkness
    prepare a death
for the flesh which sings now
makes moan and shivers silver
as the moon renews her light.

The Barbarians

If the victors were magnificent!
They are dazed by a splendour of broken palaces;
Cracked floors are the smoothest they have walked.
More beautiful than their goddess
(I have seen her in effigy, scowling)
Are our underfed women (bitches!)
                              the common girls
They keep in their quarters.

Their commander is a squat devil,
Strong and cunning in a shabby coat;
He rides the city
With an armed guard and a rumour.

I think they will stay here,
Learning the streets, picnicking by the lake.
The wind drops and the dust settles.
They will walk among old tombs
Looking for ancestors.

Medusa

Softer than padding beast, without alarm
Of conqueror's heel,
Through the stone shapes of men and animals
Which seemed, for all their fixity, to press
Towards her chair – their muscles rippling stone
To achieve the further inch –
I trod the air and came
To where she sat, the snake-wigged mask beside her.

Bronze-blue her eye and yellow-bronze her hair,
Her skin tanned deep
By the thousand-year summer
In which her eyes held me
As if she remembered at that summer's end
My shape as stone defined by her memory.
She was beautiful; she did not speak.

Fixed my feet, sword-arm numb to the shoulder.
She sat still in that stillness.

I could not kill her until she put on the mask.

John at Machaerus

The pipe yearns and she moves
the drum commands
            she is shaken;
pale arms describe in air
            the snare and net
small feet pace out captivity.

The pipe shrills
        sharp as her breasts
the drum sounds
        deep as her thigh;
she is the daughter of music
        queen of air
        and mistress of the wind.

No man comes fleet as the wind
none springs
as the body of air in air
none steps the mountain
with so light a foot
none carves the rock and sand
with touch so delicate
and swift, moves always
through eddy and involution
downsweep and leap
the caressing of earth
the prancing.
The wind is here before them
        sharp with the sand
the blind see as spinning corners of dust
and the lame, pirouetting, mimic;

and if the deaf hear
      who shall not hear
      this disturbance of air
as the dead are raised
      for the dead dance of the dead
and shrouds stream down the wind
and a reed is shaken.

The wind is here before them; the dumb are dumb;
the word is here before them, dances here,
an ignorant girl for flesh –
her body speaks
      as the crests of a storm sea
        no word but death.

And falling her body speaks
      as the wind in its great sigh;
      there is no name but mine
      there is no word but death
      in the spread limbs
      in the rasping throat
      in the vortex of still waters.

The Nihilist

Kick in the door

For some, pillage;
For some, rape.

Blood in the great beds
Bubble of urine
   Among altar-fragments

I came clod-hopping back
   down that corridor.

Neither the image
Nor the broken image
        suffices.

The Autumn–Born in Autumn

I

At morning a ballet of mist
    dawdles through the trees
    and the air is a frail arm
    relinquishing a shoulder;
We walk through stripped orchards,
    ruined courts of ripeness.
All that is to be gathered
        is gathered.

Day is a hill and a distance
    remembered through a haze
    and clear eyes clouding
    within a warmth of farewell;
We walk through stubble fields,
    the swallow is gone, the far wood
Breaks out a modish banner of rust
            and blood.

The season of our coming
    is upon us; shrunken
    the gesture at parting;
    how should we not be sad?
Under the elm and under the linden
    the nights come early estranging
Summer. That summer we slept
        in the dark.

II

Our sadness speaks as if the sun began
an elegy for summer and recalled
the burning eye of Cyclops to midheaven –
a zenith and a rage which ruled
the calm of copper noon. In our conceit
the sun remembers summer as a man
remembers his lost strength and boasts
of brawl and triumph, and the once-proud breasts.
A quaver of light syllables slurs towards sunset.

The sun laments himself in our conceit
of earth as centre, of ourselves as earth
left desolate upon a little day.
We must be mock-men and ventriloquists;
silent, the sun pursues his fiery way,
burning himself, having no need of speech.
The shadows are a dreary doubledutch,
fancy vernacular, all slang and snide –
a text which, in conceit, we would translate.

Our sadness speaks, attributing a meaning
both to the yellow leaf which waits to ride
the wind and to the sap returning to the root.
Blind in the cave of earth, by stench of burning
choked, may we achieve an elegiac tone.

As if an aftermath were a beginning.

III

Lady our first cry and our first song
– we are hence, we are gone, as though
                we had not been there –
shaped themselves once for your indulgent ear.
Again are our voices lifted
      but who will hear us now?
A girl comes to dance the year to death.

What have we sung but farewell,
      the anniversaries of exile?
Is virginity renewed in river-damps
and northwest winds?
      Mother, wearing your russet mantle
a girl comes to dance the year to death.

The yellow leaf clings to the tree
the yellow leaf goes with the wind
we slept in the dark
we shall sleep in the dark.
Dancer dancer
dance the year to death.

Theocrasy

My darling, since you still create
  The image of your god as man
And nightly kneel to contemplate
  A chaste one – petrifying Pan –

And then for satisfaction creep
  Between chill sheets, beyond all qualms,
To dream virginity asleep
  Forever in his hoary arms,

I, whom no lesser faith compels,
  Praise the goddess who hears my groan
And sets on you with wanton spells
  A likeness you dare not disown.

Ballade of the Spectre of Communism

ballistic missiles now incline
to intercontinental raid,
straight to the moon the party line
through clouds of sodium has strayed,
live communists all lands parade
and drive a ghost to haunt instead
beyond the final barricade
the dead which are already dead.

farewell to purge and plot malign
to brother killed and friend betrayed
to monolithic state and shrine
to talk of war and terms of trade
to superstructures which have swayed –
Engels and Marx await my tread
where all is withered, where are laid
the dead which are already dead.

none infiltrates to undermine
the sure foundation of that shade,
there deviating dusts combine
and in one bloc are equal made,
'jackal', 'hyena', 'renegade'
lie down together in one bed,
no dialectic has dismayed
the dead which are already dead.

kumrad do not – the colours fade,
not even you look really red –
disturb when digging with that spade
the dead which are already dead.

227 Idle Words against Apollo

I woke when dirty-fingered dawn
Swilled out the washbowl of the sky,
A streaky bacon-rasher lay
Along the east and up there spun
The sizzling fried egg of the sun,
The clangour of the kitchen-pots
Proclaimed Old Busy to his courts:
    'Breakfast and bustle, work or school,
    Each scullion to his shining task!
    Act for the hour is opportune!'
I stayed abed and slept till noon.

Like suet dumpling, heavy, dull,
A post-meridian copper disc
Sits in the stomach of the sky;
Those who have eaten here before
Will know the waiter for a queer,
That the chef sweats into the soup
And that the menu is a lie
In any language. Take a tip,
We come here to digest and die.

Father of raging thirst and dust,
Of fever-touch and stinking feet,
Lord of the blood run thin, the lust
For clarity and quick defeat,
Your priests prepare to baste and burn
(exploding cinder-bombs in turn)
The living flesh upon the bone.
Herr Ober! This is overdone.
What physicist shall play the fool
In the long afterglow of all?

I do not know if I shall write
(and bloody clouds shall be his pall)
A poem or get drunk tonight
When a cool darkness, still unslain,
Defines oblivion and the moon,
But this I prove, till day is done,

There is no poem in the sun!

The Slush

A dah dah something moon the rhyme is june
June/moon not something and I am not sure
I dream of where you are, not any more;
When I forget the words I hum the tune.

Play on; the bobby-soxers used to swoon;
New blue or something; like a metaphor
For things which other people once forswore
Which I forget and tum-ti-tum the tune.

Hey cow and diddle fingerprint the spoon;
She wears again the cloudy veils she wore,
Then, undescribed, swings naked to outsoar
All mumble, mist and memory; the moon;
New slump of silver, dead symbolic core;
I hum the tum tum something moon/June tune.

Lullaby

Soft as the shadows
    firelight throws
(This is a world that will not last)
Light as gossamer
    warm as fur.
Why does the evening wind make haste?

Soft as the shadows
    firelight throws
(Why does a shadow dance so fast?)
Light as gossamer
    warm as fur
This is a world that will not last.

Why does the evening wind make haste
    Swift as the shadows
        firelight throws?
Frail as gossamer
    fierce as fur
This is a world that will not last.

The Administration of Things

I

No days but these,
No Praesidium but this,
No silence but my own.
Drift of dead mind
In mind, noon its own spectre.
And what the dead men saw I see –
Girls on the lawn beneath a female sun,
Breasts, thighs, the prison of bright shade,
The certain shape of death.

Learn what is taught,
Learn only what is taught;
The same stiff dialect,
The revelation fixed;
Brittle as bone,
Stopped short like breath.
The whole summer archaic.

No age but this,
Shaped by the dead;
What they destroyed
   rebuilt as what they built,
A future traced in palms like parchment.
The silence mine, as if a dead man spoke
Or pondered in a sunlit interval
The dark from which he came.

II

Never clear, never simple
nor sharp in sunlight
and made straight;
long rain, a harvest rotting,
the report 'harvest rotting',
this report read, the discussion,
techniques of drying-out
and nameless fear.

Yet more approximate –
memories of an unknown;
all that a symbol masked
bare of a sudden;
a wall fallen, emptiness
an unending step.
The report read.
This read between the lines.

We move with the dead in mind.
Give us something easy to run
like Adelkhanov's shoe factory;
bankrupt shoe-makers begging for jobs,
unions hardly heard of.

III

They have found order
and they enforce order.
A frame to hold the living and the dead.

The cities content,
evening a caress:
they too seek that
– on their terms.
The crowd in the main square
– we too should disperse it.

They enforce order.
When apathy fails,
the act of fury.

They have found order.
To us a formal portrait, dark,
varnished with precedents
of dawn and death.
                    To them
– fire glints on the velvet,
   the brush-stroke lives –
a kind of reality handed over;
like an unprogrammed pleroma.

IV

She dances the dark
    a darker shadow
then any that glides
    between dusk and dawn
she dances the dark
    a remoter music
fading before her
    draws her on
into the void
    of night and silence
into the depth
    of the dark god's blindness

Naked she moves
    where she senses nothing
but death of sense
    in the cold god's cold
death of sense
    and his ears unhearing
touch taste gone
    and she too grown old
smelling her sweat
    as her body dances
making her own
    the dancing darkness

V

No days but these
Days to be lived out
The revelation fixed
The death-rate one hundred per cent.

Bitter days, brothers,
February days, a hint
of Jarrow round the gates
at noon. We have made
too many things too well
and the wrong things
and who has not slept
        on the job
and half of us
are not wanted
and rumour running says more.
Bitter days,
the work-gates at noon.
And what did Marx say?
you've forgotten,
I've forgotten.
There are no hills
we can take to.
February, fill-dyke.

VI

Riot, tumult, anticipated disturbances
or ice
or war
acts of god, enemies, pirates

at these risks

restraint of princes, rulers, peoples
quarantines, lockouts, strikes, combinations
fire on board, in hulk or craft

at this peril, these perils

or from any act, neglect, default whatsoever
or ice
or war
proceeding by any route, however circuitous
or as near thereto as she may safely get.

The wind turns and the tide waits.

Send us on something easy like a run to Ithaca.

VII

A smell of living –
dark limbs in the darkness

My hand cupped the breast
hard-nippled
and I remembered the flesh

warm thigh wet crotch
salt lips and scent of hair

Remember now thy creator
    in the night of his little death.

VIII

Sword or stealth, strength or ancient blood,
Conqueror, elect or heir – however you come,
Have no compassion. Curl the lip,
Let the eye grow cold.

Who more brutal than we
Who less compassionate
What colder eyes than ours
Who more unflinching
Facing the endless faces

Ours the command
The calm of copper noon
The Sind in blossom
An ante-natal clinic
In Deolali South

To rule: a grievous scourge.
We move with the dead in mind.
Time kills the dead,
Time and the death of memory.
A dark; simplicities
of Adieu and Anon.

IX

No way but through the night, no night but this.
An unending step, the dead in mind,
The death of memory in the dancing dark,
A silence in the valley far below.

Peak, the first air,
the drag of earth
to be learnt again
how breasts hang heavy

Descent, one sweep
of the eye, bare
ridge, wooded slopes,
mountain meadow;
down to the dark lake.

His the dark, mine the eye
like the moon in his night.

Echo

I

Except as I speak she is silent. When I speak
She answers in no accent but my own,
Makes her reply true to the last word
Repeating nothing which I have not said.
I speak and she replies. Yet her reply
Lingers upon the word as if the word
Awoke a memory of speech, of how to speak,
Not as I spoke but as she might have spoken.
I speak and she replies. My word is changed.

II

I have said: 'Mere acoustics'. I have said:
'After the word the word resounds
'In accidental halls, chance corridors,
'Briefly incongruous or briefly apt.
'And thunder in the hills
'Is mere reverberation.
'A limp scourge drags the dust,
'A whip cracks empty air'.
I have whispered in galleries contrived for answer.

III

I speak and she replies, making my word her own,
As if I spoke in the darkness of her dream
With the tenuous memory of her speech –
Delaying Saturnia with mischievous chatter,
Calling, disconsolate, down forest paths;
The pool, the broken surface,
The smooth surface unbroken.
I speak and she replies as if we met
With a caress for which there are no fingers.

IV

Here let us meet. She has heard this before.
And spoken this, though no tongue
Touch the teeth, though no lips
Shape the sound,
No living breath give voice.

Keeper of many voices, she has heard
All flesh made sigh and stanza.

And now I speak.

There is my word.
There is the interposition of silence.
There is the tremor in a flesh unmade.

Missing Persons

Just because I neither smiled nor spoke –
Letting you pass me with the saluting glance
Which any attractive woman can take as tribute –
Don't think that I didn't know you
Or that you – staring ahead,
Recognition in the corner of an eye –
Did not know me.

I was in love with you at the age of ten and kept silent.
Your hair was yellower then and longer,
You wore prettier dresses than most of the girls.
Either we share an excellent memory for faces
Or ghosts inhabit the flesh.

The Road from Kenninghall

'. . . she drew rein at Kenninghall . . .'

Out of the night
from the shuttered room
by a blind path
in the starless hazard;
man I bring darkness.

Out of the flame
which burnt alone
in the shuttered room
unquenched;
man I bring fire.

Out of the blood
(by birth by right)
so nearly spilt
so spurned;
man I bring blood.

That the faith hold
by axe and flame
in the dark land
measured by my mercy.

A Woman of the World

You know the way of the wind
and the breaking bone,
dawn like an early death;

how summer leers – a sheen
composed in a shade.
Shall I tell you

what you know? Does
the dawn-wind bow
and propose
some new truth to the rose?

I bring you a twist of thought,
a pattern-maker's whim;
the iron of your wish.
Queen of illogic
what, except what you know,
is worth the telling?

You know paths over hills
which I have not climbed.
Shall I show you the paths?

You know the curve
of the river.

How shall I lead you
through the great plains
which open behind you?

From a Provisional Capital

I

Hang-dog, amnesia–like, the air
Sags like a long–unanswered prayer,
Sprawls solidly across the town
To send blood-pressures shooting down,
And clamps an ennui, undefined,
On the blurred edge of hill and mind,
Collapsing, a besetting sin,
To seal a river valley in.

All such a climate can require
Of men is that they quickly tire
And live on sleepily, content
About a seat of government
Where a grand coalition sours
Within its temporary towers.
Here staring blankly at a page
I met my early middle age
Thinking a thought I'd thought again.
This is no country for young men.
Here memoirs mushroom in a mist
Where might-have-beens may half-exist
And automatic stanzas run
Their course beneath a clouded sun.
A perfect frame for apathy
Stretches as far as one can see:
The aftermath of blood and soil,
No KPD, no Jews in Beuel.

II

The female circle shifts, changes,
Five women, four women, six women,
I have sat there, one man alone,
Three women, two women, four women,
None of them quite past bearing,
The same faces and the changing faces,
One man alone and the bodies dust
Beyond Orel and Tarhuna.

Apartments too new
For ghosts to guess their way;
The rooms identical but differing.
I have sat there and smiled, I have seen
The circle of thickening waists.
I have missed the men
With a touch of grey at the temples
And thirty years to die.

Two women, four women, three women,
Missing the flesh gone for ever,
Alone in the sagging flesh;
I have sat, I have smiled, I have seen
The gaps in the shifting circle.
Sleep on beyond Lemberg and beyond Vinnitsa!
Shall I write your dialogue for you?
'I'm bored.
'Where are the children?
'We're going home!'

III

Cities rebuilt; like scars.
The goddess has no name.
Who but she rules, three-fold,
The thrice-divided land?
I am the barren man.

A third of alien speech,
A third of dogma, dull
With double-talk and death.
And what do they mean here?
I am the barren man.

Who but she, wholly one
And treble in intent,
Rules the divided land?
I am the barren man.
The goddess has no name.

IV

A life continued like late afternoon
After an early afternoon of love.
Why wake, why rise to sleep-walk in the sun,
Why cast the languors off?

The armies are bonemeal on the great plain,
The blood is washed from the Atlantic shallows.
What terror will be stricter than our terror?
Destruction more destructive? Who will strike?
What defence stands that was not once cast down?

Sun in my eyes, strong sunlight on the pillow.
A life continued into separation.
What further ardour can the day demand?
Wait for the dusk and hunger,
Long shadows, slanting light.
A face and breast in profile against sunset.

V

When my words have been true
                for ten centuries,
When age after age is consoled:
             'Well in that ruin
     'one at least found fortune,
     'his page embraces her still'
And in Kurdish or beyond Kumara
My words call you back from death;
And you come; and I never tire of calling . . .

Face to face, the night made flesh,
facing the dark in their place,
sprawled, lulled, sucking sweet air,
we lie in place of the dead,
named, known and knowing,
a darkness countenanced,
dawn never to come

When they seek the place
through the dark, faceless,
only knowing light has failed

When they lie in our place
their flesh made night
dawn never to come

Know then, as now,
I shall not forget.

Ten centuries true to the letter.

Love. The cold day.

VI

In Rhöndorf bleach distinguished bones,
At Dollendorf the vineyards cease;
A pond, a castle and two swans,
Bad Godesberg will keep the peace;
The river passes, flowing on,
Leaves Königswinter to the Dutch,
Skirts round a government and Bonn.
Schwarzrheindorf has a double church.
The century and season slow.
'mouth to source pure'. *Spätlese*. Tense
A great negation builds its No
From decencies of decadence.
No more. No longer. That was then.
The dark mechanics wreck the state.
The hills and villages regain
Importance for a later date.
Late, less to say; a sinking sun
Throws shadows down to meet the dusk;
Crow, charcoal, death; the colours run.
Late, less to do; I watch the mask
Of twilight fitted to the day.
A woman veiled – the eyes unseen,
The lips unkissed – who moves away.
And green is now the darkest green.
Late, less to need and less to give,
I listen where I spoke. I wait
To hear the last diminutive
That light may yet enunciate.
A wing unfolds, a line of black
Joins earth to sky upon the height.
A nameless watcher turns his back.
And silence takes the shape of night.

Some Aspects of the Goddess

for m.r.

She, the successor to the gods,
    their predecessor too,
all things to all men (this includes,
    though briefly, me and you)

is, if you like, 'pure principle',
    abstraction debonair,
to cold blank minds a merciful
    no-image in the air;

is, if you dream, the stooping form
    and phantom of delight,
clear queen of the archaic norm
    constructed in the night;

is, when the sun stands high above
    and feet are on the ground,
resembled most by girls in love.
    What more need I propound?

Before the dayspring heard his bawl
    God found, to his surprise,
A woman in the midst of all –
    whom you shall recognise.

Ballade of the Only Aspect

She who assumes the shapes of fate
which one by one we recognise
in likenesses that lacerate
and leave us stripped to scars we prize –
from metaphors beyond surmise
she steps to smile and correspond
and when I could believe my eyes
I knew her as a blue-eyed blonde.

She, all that we articulate,
she, silence, she who simplifies
the oath that we may get it straight
and then confounds our loyal lies,
once told me plainly to devise
'The shaping word shall be your bond'
an image each could visualise
'You knew me as a blue-eyed blonde'.

Were green eyes once the winking bait?
Were brown eyes once the warmer prize?
Does raven hair still stream in spate
and rustle in a night of sighs?
Such deviations I despise
my imagery pursues a fond
obedience and a single guise.
I knew her as a blue-eyed blonde.

Prince, as you stroke that red-head's thighs
and feel the living flesh respond
I know too well how hard she tries
I knew her as a blue-eyed blonde.

Chione

I wear a greatcoat in spring
A topcoat in summer
Temperature's rising
I'm getting no warmer
A snow-queen called Chione
                    is my gal.

Her love is cold
Shiver-exciting
How can I be bold
When frost-bite is biting?
A snow-queen called Chione
                    is my gal.

Eternal snows
I find very nice,
Chione knows
She's got me on ice.

I slither and slide
Past polar-bears
Only the blizzard
Tells me she cares
A snow-queen called Chione
                    is my gal.

Song of the Square Meal

Outside Dudinsk a poet sang
'The world is endless, cold and dead,
'The ice a claw, the wind a fang.'
A wolf-girl jumped into his bed.

A poet sang near Bikampur
'The world is endless, dead and hot,
'The land a corpse, the sun a jeer.'
A jackal-girl fed well that night.

Ten miles from London: 'Endless, dull
'As kitchen-hearted needlework.'
A quiet domesticated girl
Brings to bed her knife and fork.

Schoolgirls Swimming

Breaking the water with the breasts of boys
They postulate an innocence – the pool
A chlorinated oblong – prenymph noise
Crosses a width of splash and spray and ripple.

Above blue tiles they swim, white caps midwater
Bob in a dazzle; surface ornament.
Roused from a doze Hyperion and satyr,
Blinded, slump back upon the warm cement.

Beyond all angles swings the open sea;
Salt, deep, a swelling amplitude, a tide
Flooding and flowering by the moon's decree.

As she lies in her bed asleep and warm
The drowning sailor cannot tell his bride
How calm the ocean lay before the storm.

Since the War

He stands up

A wet leaf
    brushes his face
or a dry wind
    defines him

his feet
    in sand
his feet
    in mud

faraway mud
    of which we know
    nothing

He stands up
your beloved son
he moves forward

Little men
    of another colour
        kill him.

Orpheus

When I remember death

    at one with the wave,
    Tantalus;   air empty
    of wings;   the stone
    in place   in place

When I remember death

    the song leading to light
    and the feet which followed

When I remember death

I am afraid to turn my head.

Wrack

Night-labour ends and the striving;
   White waves ride to the shore
   Proud in the light.
If a girl comes from the sea
We shall name her: 'The Sea-born'.

A Greeting for Sophie Elizabeth

The cry of birth,
The smell of blood,
Small things;

Good for us,
Bad for General Motors;

Welcome to our concern.

'. . . what bites the poet?'

Dusty of coat,
Sniffing at many heels,
The same old hounds
(Red-eared as dawn)
Pick up the authentic scent.

You must be connoisseurs of screaming.

The Midday Muse

I

Faithless as light – a bright blade flashing
Between sun and water –
Her eye picks out the shadow of that blade;
Men as sons, men as lovers, men
As meaning at all – her lopping smile
Beheads these self-maimed concepts; boys race
Down the shouting beach to the rocky shallows.

Building-blocks of sunlight
Erect a simple noon –
I walk my little shadow
Out of the solid shade; hot sand
And knives of light
Define me for the hour I haunt
In which she needs no apparition.

Sea, sun and sea, the ricochet of dazzle,
Blind blue on blue, layer of light on light,
A burning mask, the hollow sockets –
So I assume the form that I am given
At noon. And fire is fire. And valid
No oath that at its taking lit the dark.

II

They all cast shadows
Even in the shadow
No shade is shade enough.

Oiled arms and backs
And shoulders, lobster-ankles;
The creamed and sticky sand.

They fade against the sun;
A bubble of fat
And then the melting bone.

A sabre-stroke of sun,
Boys hobbling across
The bloodstained rock,

Man cut down to his shadow
– A sunlit step
On a surreal beach.

III

A procession of final forms
Provides the last disguise
The form I had
The hold on nothing
The form that oblivion found.

You children of the dark
Shall describe a figure,
Constant, accessible,
Silver and cold
As deliverance.
You children of the light,
Faithless as light, shall put on
The dazzle of shadow

And burnt, dismembered boys
Shall disperse to empty air
Mimicking burning wind
    and burning sand.

IV

Empty as heaven her eye
Name the dead
Empty as air
And the wind
And the place thereof

Empty as mercy
And she shall not save
Name the dead
Blue as the summer sky
And bright as ice

Where she found form
Scars show
              Name the dead
Illustrious place-names
And men and you meet
Her eyes.
              Name the dead

V

Now of noon's mercy is the most
That all of reason shall not tell
As rose when every shadow fell
The torso of a sun-tanned ghost –

Man, lover, son. A shadow cast,
A muscled king, a certain crown.
The boys that greet him in the sun
Have carved the prow, set up the mast.

And girls shall weep to see him go
Salt tears, a spectrum-range of love,
As any goddess might approve
Or mothers in the tug of sorrow.

Now of noon's mercy is the least
That reason shall not tell at all.
A fire, a flame, a pyre, a pall,
A charred wreck drifting west or east.

Ballade of an Unforeseen Nostalgia

Repression was at its height –
even Gomulka was in prison . . .
LORD GEORGE-BROWN, *'In My Way'*

You knew just who the villains were
Because you had them on your list.
The ritual gun butt on the door,
A handcuff round the waiting wrist,
Then off in early morning mist;
It seemed as though it couldn't fail
And no one bothered to resist –
Even Gomulka was in gaol.

You knocked them down, they hit the floor
Like any kulak fatalist;
There weren't no kulaks any more
And so we took the communist.
The club and kidney kept their tryst
For deviations to curtail,
And quick as you could clench a fist
Even Gomulka was in gaol.

Things aren't like what they was before
They turned the service legalist;
Inquisitor-conspirator;
We was not ordered to desist,
The whole politburo were pissed
And innocence of no avail.
We owned the mill, we had the grist.
Even Gomulka was in gaol.

Brother, let's try to co-exist
(perhaps he's only out on bail)
And slop-out like a Bolshevist.
Even Gomulka was in gaol.

Minusland

for Sophie Elizabeth who named it

I know it well – the coast recedes
Past nothing into doom and debt,
And once ashore a low road leads
Through four days walking in the wet

To nowhere much and then turns back
Past lesser places long since gone.
Deadend dies out in cul de sac
With a sackgasse further on.

The top pop there is Nonono,
The colour films are black and white.
Thin hands relinquish all and go
To negatives beyond their night.

Alack, anonymous it lay,
I knew it ill before you came
Looking like dawn defining day
To call it by its proper name.

Stadtbahn: Early

Some bowels have moved, some stir;
Some dreams have ended well.
Some eyes still fix their stare
On headlines out of hell.

Two talkers talk to hear
What they survived to say,
Defining out of fear
The blatant shape of day.

I did not seek this dawn,
I did not want to wake,
I stand and sway and yawn,
I know of no way back.

A sleepy girl, half-dressed,
Still lathering the soap
Round an enormous breast,
Got off at the last stop.

The Man with the Red Guitar

Things as they are have been destroyed
WALLACE STEVENS

I

He plays upon his red guitar
The revolution red,

Red Flag, red star,
Rose, sunset, rust —

A solid colour in his head
Shudders upon the living strings,

The doctrine right, the dogma true,
Rust, sunset, rose —

Things as they should be beat their wings
Against the cage of judgement due,

Secret policemen, woken, curse
The vibrant backing to his verse,

Rose sunset rust —
Rust sunset rose —

He plays because he must
The instrument he chose.

II

Biermann in East Berlin, Villon unhung
          — PRAVDA

A minor Praesidium
Pales. The fiction

Of Rosa Luxemburg's
Blood; the sailors

Lenin killed. A purged
Generation, all paunch

And office-pallor –
If you own a red guitar

You can show them what they were:
Simple, brave, enthusiastic.

You dare their terror of what they were
With a little François-musik

The rope is bright and strong
But cannot throttle long

Whereat the Praesidium,
Doubling the guard, shall blanch.

III

Das sind doch alle Kommunisten

He plays upon his red guitar
A dirge of dirty red.

Mourn the lost province, touch the scar,
Bloodstains, the many dead –

For none of these can a man atone
Though he play a red guitar alone

That no one else can hear but we –
Anarchists, POUM, the ILP,

Catholics, conservatives, what we are –
The faithful praying their faithful prayer.

Grant him, if need be, heroic status –
The apparatchiks run the apparatus.

The empire fell and we know the signs.
The Reds are Reds and the Jews are Jews.

We never write more than sixteen lines
In praise of anyone but the Muse.

IV   *On the Left of the Pleroma*

What would the Muse be if he imagined her,
How would she let herself appear

Bathed in the blaze of her servant sun
(as he looked at dawn) with the East behind her,

Lips of crimson and fiery hair;
How would the revolution run

With her transilience; moon by moon,
Blood on the moon and the shattered icon:

Dancing inside a grinding glacier,
Plucking a played-out red guitar,

What could he do except imagine her –
Red as the wreck of things as they are –

Body brilliant as fire on ice,
Eyes aflame like the ice on fire –

Brought to bed by a blind desire
How should his vision not suffice?

v   *Ode to Stalin*

Master by whose command the dialectic ceased,
Great simpleton of power and death and war,

Cynic and smiler, pipe-smoking high priest
With no god left worth praying to or for,

Portrait torn down and mighty statue toppled,
A name made great and then a name destroyed,

The roaring litany of praise redoubled
And then the silence and the silent void –

Into the emptiness of things that are,
Mocking the monolith you might have made,

The twang and nagging of a red guitar
Played by a man brainwashed but unafraid

Seeks the last deviation to the centre –
An innocence like Bukharin's last sneer;

A course holds true from nothing into nowhere.

Sestina Supposed to have been Written while Waiting to Clean his Teeth

Seen in her fresh-creamed profile love
Resumes a likeness never lost,
A faithful aspect fills her glass
Where mirrored eyes are soft and true,
And when she turns to look away
We shall be standing face to face.

An endless street, the millionth face
Met, scanned and written off from love:
A look that looks to look away,
Not yet defined, already lost:
A sense of seeming to be true
Gone like a glitter in a glass.

Jockeying round I share the glass
With cottonwool that pats a face,
With shoulders, crumpled tissues. True
I see no face I do not love.
Decolleté the breasts are lost.
A lipstick smile is smeared away.

Until the water drains away,
Dry brush, capped tube, I clutch my glass;
A loser knows what must be lost.
Mistaking make-up for a face
The multitude sits dumb with love
Without intending to be true.

She, veiled by definition, true
To touch a single step away
And well within the look of love,
Lowers her eyes to mock the glass,
Looks up to meet her mocking face
And if she smiles a man is lost.

And if she frowns a man is lost,
The dust is cold, the deaths are true;
And never meeting face to face
We have already turned away
Leaving a blind and empty glass
To taunts of flesh and scorns of love.

A death-mask lost, I brush away,
A true grin foaming in the glass.
A quick face hurries off to love.

Quatrains

I

A breeze flicks back a muslin mist
    quick knives of light
Carve out the place of day
    and cut down night
The dagger and the dark
    a little death
Slowly the corpse at dawn
    turns over in delight.

II

Slow the slow hour of dawn
    what can its silver show
That twilight did not hide
    that darkness did not know
That is not resurrected
    in a breath
That lives for certain does not weep
    and will not go

III

As night is gone as steadfast moon
    and constant star
Are gone. Look in my eyes and tell me
    who we are
Before the bells beat out
    the emptiness of god
And daybreak blotches on the east
    a sky of weal and scar.

IV

Pale as the dawn your arms
        cool as the dawn your lips
But shadowed still with warmth
        your breast and hips;
Your eyes throw back the light
        and all that I possessed
I find again; and at my fingertips

V

The tense and trace of what we were
        (when two made one
Lay there oblivious
        in oblivion
Nor cared nor knew
        if life or death
Ruled that redundant shore
        and claimed us for its own)

VI

Recurs, erectile, wanting
        – day derided, day denied,
Day a cold sentry
        paces on outside;
But our relief is here
        our calling and our care;
We come again
        and here
                again
                        upon a single tide.

VII

We shall not drown upon this ebb.
    Doze, dally, drift,
Lie still, bearing and borne,
    feel the long lift
Of death mid-ocean touch us
    in the shallows. Not on this ebb,
Fighting for breath, cast forth,
    caressed by wind and spindrift.

VIII

Here is dry ruin and a fallen tower,
    a jellied bone
Cools after sear and shock.
    A sigh or moan
Would be the whole of truth,
    sweet sigh
        the whole of truth:
Scar, aftermath and silenced bird
    and in that desolation

IX

No name, no numbered year,
    no palpable event,
No sign in passing
    meaning what was meant;
The phantom of a world
    left as it is,
Seen as it was by men
    with nothing to lament –

X

But we
      arise my love
            are doomed to day . . .

Invitation

Walk with me through the afternoon
In the wind that calls the leaves;
Soon the leaves will yellow
And go with the wind.
We have been here before. Walk with me
Like an echo through absence.

Retreats to Reality

I *Old Soldiers*

To describe what seems about to disappear
We lean here, glass in hand, mastering a slur,
Watching reflections in an old pub-mirror
Where silver flakes away behind gold-lettered glass.
The barmaid's assertive breasts, a rail of brass
Support certain points of a balance become precarious.

Bits have been shot away. What we see best is the scar
On what is left; a redefinition of much forever
Hazy; like the man to the right – a dark leer
With no profile. What we must do is wait
For intangibles to touch and then re-state
The barmaid, say, as a naked form of fate.

Up the blanks and voids! We have not turned away.
We are comrades in the grip of doomy day
Marching to something more than we can say.
Moscow re-imagined on an iced-in horizon
Looms as we look. Lurching to reconquer what is gone
We join in the song of the frostbitten nipple and the iron
     winter goes on.

11 *Exiles*

We dreamed of home as it was and as we were,
Thronging the known streets with the never-dead
As if all had not been lost and we were where
We had always been meant to be; the bay spread
Before us below the wooded hill, the trees we looked over
Lopped to preserve the view – to whelm in fire and blood
And mount again the nightmare of departure.

Then we went back as we are to what is there:
Strangers live out the lives we might have led
Uneasy on alien streets in the restless stir
The displaced achieve – history clutched, houses unpainted,
Graves ploughed in. Leafy branches obscure
The view of the bay from the hill. Needing no guide
We sought what we found. Returned to our exile here

We dream of home as it was and as we are,
As it is and we were; all that we lost and had
Is given again and taken, relinquished and held dear;
The dead smile and are present, we greet the living dead,
And then in this milder winter – bare branches, the bay seen
    from afar –
Turn in our certain sleep, no time and place denied,
Racing for home between nightmare and nightmare.

III   *Lovers*

A single sheet thrown aside in sunlight;
The naked bed. Nothing illicit
Drains day with a hasty gulp. Limbs
Like long syllables loll and lull by right
And turn again to what they do, content
With one vast open vowel; which rhymes.

There is no order in time consonant
With eternity. We are here to reach and grasp;
What has come, incomparable, goes in an instant;
A goddess groans, cherubim lisp,
Open mouth mouths open mouth and the word
Is flesh; cry thrusts to spasm and the spasms gasp.

A definition fits what was felt to be blurred.
We come as close as we have ever been.
What we can say, more precise than what we have heard,
Is that love is enough, never done. The grave of love is green
And we come like the dead – charred branches, the blazing
    grove –
Naked in a single sheet to the tended grave of love.

After the Economy

I

Shoulders hunched at the wind
We walk to work in the dark
For the foul wage we are glad to get.
What is sold is sold pound by pound
At prices we cannot pay.
Dawn defines dawn, day breaks
Like the nil of nought per cent.

II

What we do we do well,
Pointlessly; and because we must.
At the command of men
With minds
         like Bangladesh.

III

Nothing for nothing.
Nothing brought
Into this world.

Nothing worth having
Worth what it costs.

Dead statisticians
Numbered us.

The rest was finance.

IV

All wealth comes from the womb.
Like nothing on earth the price
Wise virgins promise to pay.

V

Now we have next to nothing.
Now we must work and want.
Now we must squander ourselves.

We walk to work.

Skeleton Speech

Ha worm. You strip the bone
   but leave the bone.

Wasserburg

for Ruth

Church at the water's edge;
Stone thrusts, lake bellies.
The moon comes marrying
Stone and water.
The drowned and the dry dead
Lie together.

We the one flesh
We the lithe lengthening
We of the clasp and kiss
We the slow coming,
Moonlight defines us
Leaving no mark
Lending a likeness.

Out on the lake
Bodies we borrowed
Sink in the moonlight.

A fish leaps silver
From the chancel
Of the lake,
Slithers across the altar.

And a Merry Meeting

for p s

I know you as you know me as I was
And as you knew me I remember you,
Making you out beyond resemblances –
A lasting likeness, to no tense untrue.

You know me as I knew you as you were
For once we walked where nothing might not be
And each face had a name and place forever
As I remember you remember me.

Thirty-five years, the kiss of recognition.
When next we meet I pray you bow your head
In a left profile bright as resurrection;
I shall be leaning forward out of dread
To hear a rumour rouse oblivion:
Time is not time nor any dead man dead.

In the Eyes of the People

I *The Common View*

To see as they do, trust the tricky eye
To pick a lustre, reimpose a sheen,
Sink to reflection in a play of light;
A sleight of shadow patching up compassion.

To watch as they do, see what they are shown.
No cold voyeur, watching them as they watch,
But sharing gathered dusk or curtained day
Transfixed before the common spectacle –
If, stocky, humble, they invest the dark
With symbols, glowing, making dark symbolic,
I shall stare with them, seeing what they see:
Faces made up, invented smiles;
Visuals of gaudy panoply a screen,
A rose insists, a snake of coloured lights . . .

Blood and grimace; the bodies in the snow;
Bitten by sun and wind, the bodies in the sand;
The sprawl and lying still; the eye heroic,
Unmoved as street-scenes rock; men running
Into focus and the hand-held shot of slaughter.

Vistas of suntan, freckle, mole and scab;
A running sore as continuity.
Wrinkle, crease, scar,
Fat in its hanging folds,
Chilblain and Bengal rot, pustule and alopecia.

Attend on beauty, she is rare enough,
And with a single smile deceives the world.
At this extreme, this norm, the killers kill.

Hammered by sounds that simulate a voice –
The light on land and sea, the common day
Sealed up, indecent, in a private vision –
They ape the deed, slumped down before the scene.

I shall sit with them till they look away.

II *A Personal Appearance*

Over-rehearsed I watch the afternoon
Exploit a brightness like a faded blonde.
Damp air stagnates upon a yellow leaf,
Cold water slaps the stone –
She in a rinse of sunlight stirs the shade.
My shadow blackens,
Bleach of sea and sun;
Summer still there
Defining limbs
Still rising from the foam,
And I, pot-bellied, there to oil the tan,
Kneeling beside aloof and yielding flesh.

Cold water slaps the stone. A sudden likeness
Lost in a glass that darkens and denies.
She came, she went, I saw her clearly then.
A varnished face alive in candle-light
I stared with painted pupils from a wall
And she laughed on
Faithless beneath my frown.

The water's edge,
The flake and fall of leaves;
Swirl and deceit out in the patchy mist.
Expert in Autumn's trick exteriors
It should be simple and it should be seen
As if Narcissus, counting wrinkles, come to drown,
And seeing nothing of himself, muttered in close-up:
'The form is woman and the shape is day.'

III *For the Rehabilitation of N. I. Bukharin*

And now the tongues, lick-spittle, rook you out
Tasting the rotting cavity of silence;
Favourable mention on a stinking breath.

As if it had not been masterly, played for sneers –
Not a shop-steward in the hand-picked hall
But had not, being present, resolved on death.
The sense of a distant audience; snarling factory meetings.

That was how they see when they do not see;
That was what they do blindly when they are told;
That was the darkness that they make of darkness.

And now they spew you, tentatively, up;
Trusting the afterlight in which they live.
As if when all the surfaces were sealed,
The quiet grave closed, the meaning caught elsewhere,
A broken body broke the breaking wave.

IV   *Facing the dark*

for Ruth

Here are the shadows,
An horizon burnt to ash,
Dusk feeling forward,
        claiming form

Like a wind, touch and go
From nowhere, defining
Like dead flame. Shifting
        blotches deepen.

Who would turn back
To the ring of light,
The bright cell? Lost
        contours

Beckon. A darkness
Going out to meet
The darkness, trusting
        fatigue,

The limit of the day,
I am the shadow
Beside you in
        the shadow.

And first we see
What shade has made
Of shade. Then nothing
But the night, heartbeat
        on heartbeat.

Sclerosis

I

A dusk before the dark,
a clank of armoured cold,
dull words unmeant to mark
a meaning left untold

to no-one; braincells dead,
arteries almost blocked,
an echo in the head
of doom gone off half-cocked.

The watching eyes are bright;
pale lips and mauve-rinsed curls
make up by dying light
a dream of wrinkled girls.

A silence before silence
as if a thought went on
and shudders yielded sense
although the mind is stone.

II

Remember nothing and remember this
remember nothing then remember never
kisses beyond recall in any kiss
molten virginities burnt out forever

Remember knowing nothing ever known
remember knowing nothing known again
the cringe of being in a cold dimension
the call of coming in deflowered disdain

Do not remember then remember why
there was no more than all there is no more
than painted eyes made up to catch the eye
than silken skin to cover and ignore

Remember nothing and remember how
all shall be said with nothing left to say
ice on the pane the breath's unbroken vow
when night and nothing mock the breaking day.

III

After shifts of night unslept –
no-one keeping watch in nowhere
waiting for day not to break

I have seen a dawn that crept
leprous up a silver stair
like a dead man wide awake.

Nameless faces fill the day,
strangers fated to survive;
none I know or wish to know.

Few I know are left alive,
faceless names are fled away.
Few who knew me know me now.

Now forgotten one by one
faceless name and nameless face
mock me into empty age

summon up remembering

and the kiss no more a kiss
and the shape of nothing done
and the dead to crowd the page.

I am nothing more than this.

CODA

Fatal time, mortal fate,
Old and too old.
Bright eyes blank in the cold.
Late and too late.

A Roman in Cologne

Lucius Poblicius,
old sweat –
not sculpted
as an old sweat –
standing between
the pillars
of his monument
his own monument
brought into
this museum
re-erected
his pillars
his blocks
of sandstone
48 feet high –
lark-high,
the only one
of the Fifth
to make it –
up there,
the scroll
the gown
the glory,
the spotlight on him
all the way
from Teretina until now.

Death Valley

Haze on the hazy hill,
pinewoods in the haze;
grapes on the vine still.

They die under the Drachenfels
in high fog, in brown
scum above high fog,
they die
below the Petersberg
in layer on layer
of mist, in a built-in catarrh.

Pines on the hill,
poplars by the river;
no horned skull
in the sand
nor a naked sun
nor desolation;
they stifle here
in air the Romans breathed.

You can die here watching
a splintered pillar of sun
collapse through mist and morning
and topple into the river –
a slump of silver,
then the solid gold.

Haze on the hazy hill,
the vine still, the grape.
The apple rots where the apple fell,
a far shore takes shape.

The Lighted Castle

Clear autumn and a harvest moon,
The flood-lit castle on the hill,
A sense of nothing lost and gone;
An hour that has not come to kill

Delays, sustains us as we are,
At ease, we scarcely hear the chime;
A picture-window shows each star.
The time when we shall tire of time

Is not yet now and not yet here –
No clot of cloud, no skylike stain,
No sense of nothing coming near
On wet black stones in icy rain.

Farewell

You gave me life
and you are dead
No tongue
but the tongue
you taught me
saddens the air
to lament you

Mother
the pain done
and the awful
ache of bone
Mother
the glass dark

Your blue eyes
scorned the day

You gave me life and I am glad
that you are dead
You gave me life
and I am glad
that I shall die.

Sestina at the End of Socialism

We watch the workers walk away,
We hear a time-clock punched in time.
The whole account is in the red
But not much in the shops today.
Ruin is coming like a rhyme.
The party is as good as dead.

The leadership as bad as dead,
Frightened and too old anyway.
A gut that rumbles makes a rhyme
For something being sick in time.
Old men wake up to dread the day,
The mockery of dawn is red.

'The People's Flag is crimson-red,
It flutters o'er our martyred dead'
We shall not sing that song today.
Massed choirs no longer voice the way
Men massed might make a sense of time
Surpassing reason with a rhyme.

A dogma ruthless as a rhyme;
The sodding tundra sodden red,
Kulak and gulag, slime and time,
Purge/urge, the duty to be dead.
Ten million roubles bet each way.
The lads are eating horse today.

It could be my last day today —
Young Rubashov will know the rhyme
Eternity might shrug away.
The girls were young, the wine was red,
And hardly anybody dead.
Perhaps there'll be another time.

At some small rotting point in time
This is the end of yesterday;
A future waiting for the dead.
The rhyme is only there to rhyme.
The autumn comes, the leaves turn red.
Ungood the leaves are blown away.

Tick-tock, Ingsoc, a load of rhyme.
Expletive day, deleted red.
Dead end. Dada. Go out this way.

Confrontation

If he were god he would
forgive us and come down.
We nailed him up to see.

The crown of thorns in place
he hung there on the tree
with blood all down his face.

A long spear stabbed his side.

God hates the human race.

Triolet

I went to kiss you and you turned away.
You would not let me kiss you on your lips.
I kissed your cheek and knew my lips were clay.
I went to kiss you and you turned away
Into some locked dimension of the day.
You hear the scrabble of my fingertips.
I went to kiss you and you turned away.
You would not let me kiss you on your lips.

Triolet

You are still beautiful by candlelight.
I watch you eagerly across the room
Seeing each wrinkle smoothed, each puff pulled tight.
You are still beautiful by candlelight,
A Miners Liquid Makeup of delight.
My skin is parchment and my dark is doom.
You are still beautiful by candlelight.
I watch you eagerly across the room.

For You, Ruth

When I am I only as you recall
me to your mind where else I may not be
more than a name on stone a paper scrawl
leaving lost things my only legacy

when when is then and then you think of me
sleeping for good where night and never sprawl
open a dream a crack and you will see
how quick I come if I can come at all

and if and where and when are now and here
I shall be up that instant from the shade
finding a track that will not fade from view
racing along to be a man remade
blinking bright light away outstripping fear
and coming to see you and only you.

City

Thin-walled
junk sound
crash-vista
of fame

where we
did not
dwell

and where
we died

inhabiting
no love

nor knowing
one in a million
by his name.

Folkestone

There is nothing between the sleepless night
and the breaking wave but
gardens,
a Victorian street,
The Leas
the cliff
the shingle

and the herring-gulls'
broken electric guitar –
whinge, shriek and scream

There is nothing on the climb back
from the breaking wave but
salt feathers

The Grand

spread wings

The Metropole

and unending cries
and endless awakenings.

Frinton

Within the Gates
the numbered avenues
paved with cold
silence

No coaches
trippers
pubs
fish and chips

We have seen
the sun rise and age
and the moon set
within the Gates
in an avenue
situation

Walton and Clacton
beyond the pale

Connaught Avenue
runs from the Gates
to the Greensward
and the Greensward
stretches to heaven and
  you can see the sea.

The Late Late Later

daydreams melting into midnight
Linda Darnel Larraine Day
girls immortal in a moonlight
long ago and far away

flesh made celluloid uncarnal
ladies lost to touch and taste
Larraine Day and Linda Darnel
now forever unembraced

shadows in a brighter shadow
speak the lines they have to say
far away and long ago now
Linda Darnel Larraine Day

Larraine Day and Linda Darnel
racing clouds across the moon
midnight in a time eternal
long ago and very soon

The Flickering Shadow Stanzas

Into the unlit room like non-existence
Dusk sidles like a glimpse of the unseen;
Shadows of likeness welcome all pretence
To a dimension that has never been;
I sit alone, the light behind me dies.
Dusk packs the empty corners of the room –
A darkish girl, deception in her eyes –
With complicated light and simple gloom.

Nothing was brighter than the light of day,
Warm sun, quick wind and water on the skin,
A world of blonde and blue and things to say,
White foam and further out the silver fin
And further still horizon without end,
The light that always was on land and sea –
An honest girl on whom you can depend –
Showing what is as what was meant to be.

Here the dead lived and here they learned to die
Relinquishing the sunlight and the shade,
The picture window and the empty sky;
Feeling a tremor in a flesh unmade,
Evening and heartbreak, dusk and not to be,
They paid attention and devoted breath
To learning truly, seeing it was she,
The simple lesson taught by Lady Death.

And evening comes again with evening light,
A fading of the last of fading days.
From where I sit I watch a wall of white
Washed by a dappling of blues and greys,

The sideboard empty and the bookcase dark
With apprehension on an unread page –
On bitter lips where kisses missed their mark –
Of metaphors for ending of an age.

I need no bright eruption in the sky.
I do not want a sunset at my back,
Like the abortion of the century,
Dripping down double-glazing, bloody-black.
It is enough to sit and sit and watch
The twilight like a pause still going on
When all there was has dwindled to a blotch
As big as earth and all of time has gone,

Drained off in happy hours or leaked away,
Void as a ten-ounce tonic's chilly clink,
Opaque as barmaids' eyes at close of play –
Lost vintage, thirsty girls, the final drink:
Add to one third of Beefeater Dry Gin
Bols Orange Curaçao, one third, ice,
Then mix a third of dry white vermouth in,
Shake. 'Cherry?' 'Mead's Old Gold.' 'Oh, this tastes nice!'

Once there was firelight but the fire is out
Where once there danced the dance of naked flame
And lissom forms of lovers played about
Until the proper point of darkness came.
And once soft oil-lamp light touched cheek and hair
Calming the room in which the light was shed,
And everyone I loved was sitting there
Until a candle took me up to bed.

Night will be dark with all the daddy-gods
Cuddled together in the big nurse arms,
A snoring clutch of idle odds and sods
Dreaming of sacrifice and prison-farms.

I am what each creator could create
Blowing on any clay with any breath;
A pigmy undershadowed by his fate,
A poison dwarf who puts himself to death.

One could take half a tranquilliser now
To keep one steady as one checked the kit
Placed within easy reach, all in a row,
To make quite sure that one had all of it:
The travel-sickness pill, the final snack,
The sleeping pills and, like an airtight vault,
The plastic sack inside the plastic sack –
He died of Neodorm and Single Malt.

The definition that a shadow seeks
Is no redefinition of the light,
A sunlit radiance of snowcapped peaks
Seen naked by sheet lightning at night –
A bride in black with all the pallors pale,
Sombre mulatto bridesmaids, swarthy page,
The bride behind a never-lifted veil
And Africa a bridegroom in a rage.

My Lady Death that you were Lady Love
And Lady Mother and the night is new
And all shapes change and stars will shine above
And I shall never take my leave of you,
I thank my lucky stars unfixed by fear
Except the fear of death and being dead
That love has come again to find me here
And heap a mother's mercy on my head.

The unborn ranks of sons and daughters bow
Safe in the faint pleroma of their choice,
Eternally to be unfathered now,
Forever uncalled home by any voice

Echoing emptily across a lawn
Into a garden where a child might hide.
Night is what stands between the dusk and dawn.
No-one sees nothing on the moon's dark side.

Into the non-existence of a room
Long unseen shadows crowd to take the place
Of faceless men long gone to faceless doom,
A last light falls upon the human race.
And following the light the dark comes quick,
A black lid closes on a bloodshot eye,
And to the sound of someone being sick
A negro steals the sunset from the sky.

Invocation

The words are falling into place
Telling that you again return
As lucid as the shape of grace
The words are falling into place
Telling me I shall see your face
Where wildfires run and rumours burn
The words are falling into place
Telling that you again return.

A Dozen Villanelles

Villanelle of the Final Whole

for WJC

	★
Horrible feet and horrible teeth	*teef*
The corn uncut and the biter bit	
Old age is often a time of death	*deff*
The sort of day when you can't quite breathe	*breev*
When you can't quite stand and it hurts to sit	
Horrible feet and horrible teeth	*teef*
Something is happening underneath	*underneef*
The underneath that you daren't admit	
Old age is often a time of death	*deff*
A rusty sword as you catch your breath	*breff*
An icy stone in the stomach's pit	
Horrible feet and horrible teeth	*teef*
This is the sky you lived beneath	*beneef*
Pressing you down beyond remit	
Old age is often a time of death	*deff*
This is a grave and this a wreath	*wreef*
This is about the end of it	
Horrible feet and horrible teeth	*teef*
Old age is often a time of death	*deff*

★ *rhymewords in native tongue*

Villanelle of the Last Gasp

Put out the final cigarette
And do you really want that drink
Prepare to live and die in debt

The day is drained beyond regret
The glass is cracked the ashtrays stink
Put out the final cigarette

A dirty shirt a losing bet
You are not worth a jockey's wink
Prepare to live and die in debt

Whisky like water wet and wet
A cashflow on the rocks clink clink
Put out the final cigarette

The bedclothes will be wet with sweat
Pink elephants will all be pink
Prepare to live and die in debt

This lady dressed in stockinet
Will pour your whisky down the sink
Put out the final cigarette
Prepare to live and die in debt.

A Villanelle on Hold

I wrote a poem yesterday
naked as her next of kin
I shan't do very much today

With words as bright as breaking day
diamond nipple, scented skin
I wrote a poem yesterday

My lines still hold that fair array
Fräulein Flender smooth as sin
I shan't do very much today

In metaphors for come what may
Mrs Perkins drowned in gin
I wrote a poem yesterday

My time is lost beyond delay
virgin in a crinoline
I shan't do very much today

That's it then at the close of play
scaly hands are cold and thin
I wrote a poem yesterday
I shan't do very much today

Villanelle of the Unslept Night

A rainy wind will lash the pane
And I shall listen where I lie.
I shan't get back to sleep again.

I'll lie and hear the old refrain
Of empty buses going by.
A rainy wind will lash the pane.

Then up and out to slash and strain
And back to groan and snort and sigh:
I shan't get back to sleep again.

Noise and nocturia. In vain,
Like a relentless lullaby,
A rainy wind will lash the pane.

Some bits of night may still remain,
The dreamy bits where people die.
I shan't get back to sleep again

Before the dirty stain of dawn
Before I've even closed an eye
A rainy wind will lash the pane
I shan't get back to sleep again.

Villanelle of the Sudden Twinge

I felt the pain once more.
It may well go away.
It went away before.

A pang of something sore,
An echo of decay.
I felt the pain once more.

An achey pain, cocksure
Of coming night and day.
It went away before.

It creeps back to recur
Or jabs back in to stay.
I felt the pain once more.

The pill and shot and smear
All help and you can pray.
It went away before.

It gets to be a bore
But I can only say:
It went away before
I felt the pain once more.

An Unrhymed Villanelle

A villanelle without a rhyme
A clock that ticks no tick but tock
Like decommissioning the wheel

A massive miss a screeching brake
The mainspring snaps the hands stand still
A villanelle without a rhyme

It isn't true it can't be done
A clock that tells the time too late
Like decommissioning the wheel

The dark mechanic stops to stare
A clock that tells no time at all
A villanelle without a rhyme

The dark mechanic gets to work
I just don't care I just can't watch
Like decommissioning the wheel

Men shuffle down deserted roads
A dead sound on the stroke of ten
A villanelle without a rhyme
Like decommissioning the wheel.

A Double Villanelle

I have decreed the fortyeight hour day
And each dark hour shall lengthen thy delight;
The tempo is tomorrow's long delay.
My law of leisure idles time away
Making eternity an *Ewigkeit*;
Enjoy the whole of it on double pay.

You shall no longer live in disarray
Of fleeting moments or of sudden fright,
I have decreed the fortyeight hour day;
A minute circles like a bird of prey,
Hovers unswooping in a slowflap flight;
My law of leisure idles time away.

The status quo stands where it is to stay
For twice the time you ever thought it might.
The tempo is tomorrow's long delay
And clocks that you no longer need obey
Strike 'Never' in the middle of the night;
Enjoy the whole of it on double pay.

Who would not be immortal let him pray
To such swift gods who speed him from his plight.
I have decreed the fortyeight hour day –
A lump of time to play and then replay,
All out, stumps drawn, but no result in sight.
My law of leisure idles time away.

Dawn, double-spaced, has dawdled till midday
And luncheon found no end of appetite,
The tempo is tomorrow's long delay.
Unchanged, unaltered, not a hair turned gray,
Running to length in all you ever write –
Enjoy the whole of it on double pay.

A double villanelle, a negligée
Concealing nothing from a second sight.
I have decreed the fortyeight hour day.
The tempo is tomorrow's long delay.
A double villanelle and come what may
All loves endure, eternal flames burn bright;
My law of leisure idles time away,
Enjoy the whole of it on double pay.

Villanelle: A Blotted Weltanschauung

I only had my reading glasses on
And what I saw was quite a way away
And when I looked again the lot had gone.

I should have seen the whole thing seen as one
By eyes that flash beyond a dying day;
I only had my reading glasses on.

One steadfast gaze in detail might have done
To shape the scene. I blinked; a blinding ray;
And when I looked again the lot had gone.

What is believed is seen, the world is won
By eyes that pierce the distance like dismay.
I only had my reading glasses on.

What meets the eye is what the seer soon
Proclaims as faith. I felt a faith decay.
And when I looked again the lot had gone.

The naked girl was breasted like a swan
As my wife saw and as I heard her say
I only had my reading glasses on
And when I looked again the lot had gone.

A Phantom Villanelle

slender
fine
tender

attend her
shrine
slender

send her
shine
tender

defender
thin
slender

splendour
wine
tender

surrender
mine
slender
tender.

Villanelle of the Last Lap

walking the final mile
with nothing left to say
smiling a toothless smile

one man in single file
trying to lose his way
walking the final mile

meeting a crocodile
of schoolgirls all gone grey
smiling a toothless smile

going on all the while
to while all time away
walking the final mile

claiming no domicile
drawn on beyond dismay
smiling a toothless smile

beyond the broken stile
stumbling back to stay
walking the final mile
smiling a toothless smile.

A Villanelle in Memory of Edward Mummery

You sail beyond the setting sun,
Hold course towards the final shore.
The water and the world are one.

Daring the dark to face alone
Uncharted seas uncrossed before
You sail beyond the setting sun.

A wind that tears, the tides that run,
A broken wave, the stormy roar,
The water and the world are one.

Above pearl eyes and coral bone,
The oozy depths, the mermaid's lure,
You sail beyond the setting sun.

You are the man you made your own.
The land is drowned to dry no more.
The water and the world are one.

You make the voyage, never done,
To morning like a golden door.
You sail beyond the setting sun.
The water and the world are one.

A Badly Bloated Villanelle

A truth that we shall never know
In words we do not want to hear,
A sort of deafened inner ear,
A dumb man telling us to go
Or asking, worse, *why are you here?*
In syllables of sudden fear –
The sort of thing that scares a crow.

A conversation burning low,
A smoking wick, a sooty smear,
Dark corners out of which might peer
A truth that we shall never know.
There used to be a chandelier
And hanging from it with a sneer
A dumb man telling us to go.

A silence full of fallen snow,
An emptiness from far to near,
Then something poking like a spear,
The sort of thing that scares a crow;
A black box with a built-in veer,
A caw not sounding quite sincere,
A truth that we shall never know.

Guides and good shepherds here below
– but now the rhyme begins to blur –
A soulless psycho-engineer,
A dumb man telling us to go,
A blind man teaching us to steer,
And then that crippled mountaineer,
The sort of thing that scares a crow.

A great negation drowns our 'No'.
This ocean where we reach no shore
Was charted by a gondolier.
A truth that we shall never know
Is washed away as mermaids cheer
At wrecks and rocks and disappear.
A dumb man telling us to go

Does it with gestures showing how
To make a bonfire of the year
And pile up in a triple tier
The sort of thing that scares a crow,
A truth that we shall never know,
A dumb man telling us to go.

Bearings

It takes a blonde to break your heart.
A lean brunette will get you down.
A redhead turn and hate the sight
Of something she could tear apart.
The other girls will only bite.
A lean brunette will get you down.
It takes a blonde to break your heart.

Triolet

Young girls explode with things to say.
An older woman means the most.
Her calm assurance points the way
(Young girls explode with things to say)
To light the fuse to stir the clay –
A depth-charge like the Holy Ghost.
[(Young girls explode with things to say)]
An older woman means the most.

In the Bleachery

I

a yellow of yellow grins,
lips twisting to frame
the denture;

a red
of sunset
after sunset;

blue,
black
with thunder –

primary colours
lived in the drench
of light, died
with the light.

II

a yellow
of toothless
grins;

red of a sun
unrisen;

blue of the
blind eye –

now come the counter-colours,
into breath-thin air,
darkening the darkness.

Kenneth Cain

'. . . the squads will be armed
with airguns and bows
and arrows . . .'
Kenneth Cain
at ten
telling me
at ten
Kenneth Cain
hair no fairer
than mine
but with a curl
Kenneth Cain
expounder of straightforward
fantasy

Kenneth Cain
armed as a pilot
Fleet Air Arm
killed as a pilot
Kenneth Cain

Losses 2002

'... you three boys ...'

Norman
(youngest)
10 January
Hamilton
New Zealand

Dennis
(midmost)
2 March
Croxley Green
England

leaving me
(eldest)
dateless
nowhere

Karfreitag

The Sentences of Death

NINE ASPECTS
OF A SYNDROME

'To be taken to the place from which you came ...'

One: *Set Up*

The night is lit
as eternity
will be lit

Muse
silver shadow
Moon
silver substance

Now death is dumb

No dark sayings
dreary
the night
with dreams
of dawn
No sweaty echoes
of a broken vow
shake down
the stars

The night is lit
once and for all:
dead or alive
the night is no man's now

Moon
your leafless
windless silver

Muse
the silver
of your silence

The night is lit
for eternity
Shadow and substance
share the silver bed:
this is as good as death

There is no rhyme
for silver.

Two: *Death as a Foreign Language, Lesson One*

You will die
He will die
She will die
They will die

You are dying
He is dying
She is dying
They are dying

You shall die
He shall die
bunion
onion
She shall die
They shall die

You are dead
Twentyfour
Sixtyfour
He she they
are dead

They are the dead

In a short time
the pupil will be saying:

'a dead man
and a moonless sky'
or be pronouncing:
'the faint stale glitter . . .'

An easy language to learn.
Simple to translate.

Three: *Cowardice in Face of the Blank Page*

Words fall from lipless lips, leaves fall from leafless trees;
a bare branch, a gallows, sky a hollow socket
unstaring from a skull; echoes of guilty pleas,
claims to the right to die, fill corridor and court.

To become no one again and nothing again,
to revert to the inert start, to the cold lump
of clay crumbling to dust out on the great plain
beyond knowing, past caring, before the high jump

of forever grounded forever and no day;
no word audible, unsaid, lipless lips, unheard,
these are the leafless leaves falling, this is the way
silence begins and ends, pitiless and absurd.

You will not hear though you think you hear or could hear
if you were near enough to hear – calls of farewell
torn to whispers by a wind; high-pitched cries of fear
stifled, cushioned; interminable tales still to tell

but not to be told. You did not miss what was said
for nothing was said. You need not misunderstand
Death saying nothing (except perhaps to the dead).

There is no distant drum, no anthem, no lost land.
You will hear nothing. Do not listen until you must.
Black-capped Death believes all sentences are just.

Four: *Local Colour Seen as Camouflage*

Walking about Bad Godesberg
Waiting to die: up the hill
To the woods, through the woods,
Down the hill past the empty shops,
Past the empty department store
– when the government goes
this will be a ghost town
and I shall be a ghost.

Walking through Bad Godesberg
Waiting for death
– 'of which we know nothing' –
Strolling through town
Down the avenue to the river.

If the Rhine were the Styx
I could take the Dollendorfer ferry
– a cheerful Charon here –
To the Deadland of Niederdollendorf
And walk south through the Hades
Of Königswinter and return
on the slow Königswinterer ferry
– a sullen crew there –
To this Left Bank and Mehlem

And all would be known
– '. . . bloke back from the dead' –

The Hotel Dreesen looks up.
The Hotel Petersberg looks down.

Five: *And Daylight Hours Tomorrow*

Suicide weather
slack and dull
wrapped like a sack
around the skull
Melancholia
gnaws the bone
dine together
die alone

Just the weather
for suicide
blind and blank
like a self denied
Day was a wank
and night a nigger
a rotting rope
and a rusty trigger

Suicide weather
cold and cruel
end of a tether
end of it all
Bloody final
a soul uptight
phantomising
the real dark night.

Slack and dull
blind and blank
cold and cruel.

Six: *In the Epitaph Section*

Skull-sleep:
All that is left
Is more than we thought.

Skeleton-stretch:
Words on a page
In a closed book,
Words on a stone
In nowhere.

Bone fingers fumble
For the place,
Finding the words.

Read them as the dead read;
Let the sockets see.

Seven: *Drill for a Deathbed*

Face death
Turn to the wall
Death has no face
no fingers to touch
no hand to take
no eyes to meet
Turn to the wall

Dead or alive
as real or unreal
as you ever were
Turn to the wall
Face death
Now the man who was
not killed then
dies now

Death does not want
to be faced
nor to be understood
Turn to the wall
Death has learned no language

Look away
Face the wall
Do not wait for words.

Eight: *Sitrep*

The dead are safely dead.
We still have risks to take.
A hazard for each head.
The dead are safely dead.
Blockhead and loggerhead
Our hearts will ache and break.
The dead are safely dead.
We still have risks to take

And promises to break.
The dead are true to death,
We still have time to fake
And promises to break
And so for no one's sake
We draw another breath.
Unsworn to ache and break
The dead are true to death.

We shall lie safe and true
In undawns yet to break
No dying left to do
We shall lie safe and true
As doubly dead and two
With nothing to forsake
We shall lie safe and true
In undawns yet to break.

The dead are safe and sure.
We flinch and fear the dark
And names that mean no more.
The dead are safe and sure.

Water from shore to shore
And nowhere to embark.
The dead are safe and sure.
We flinch and fear the dark.

The dead are safely dead.
The dead are true to death.
The dead are safe and sure.

Nine: *Fade Out*

The night is lit
cunningly

Her eyes meet his
his arms hold her

Shadows,
they kiss in the shadow

They are lit
for the final scene
and eternity
(silver and silver)
This is their moment
monumental
they clutch forever

There will be nothing
after this
No proof that
you were her
or I was he
No rhyme for silver

A small night music
ends. Death follows
dark and dumb.
Like a man in love.

This is no place for us.

The Poetry of Matthew Mead

MATTHEW MEAD has said that 'the important poem by a contemporary is, for me, Sabais's *Generation*.' This poem, which Mead and his wife have translated, records the life of a German whose adolescence was the years of the Third Reich, and whose introduction to manhood was the Wehrmacht's eastern front:

> Our best cogitations dwell
> in the rotted shin-bone that a peasant,
> far away on the Dnieper,
> far away on the Elbe,
> tosses from his field . . .

and further in the same poem Sabais speaks of himself as one of the survivors who 'sometimes . . . forget those two who / rot for the third'. In the introduction to his translation Mead has commented,

> The capital letter abstractions – Beauty, Love, Courage – are redefined by reference to incidents in war. The survivor cannot be certain that the past will remain the past. The present details of moneymaking and manufacture can be managed, as can the cocktails and canapés of the social round. But the present has much of an aftermath about it and there is always the feeling of being 'never quite thawed out' and the possibility of a surrealistic lapse into something which will, perhaps, never be done with. As a member of Sabais's generation I find his poem accurate. He presents the experience of that generation without self-pity, rhetoric, anger or blame. The difference between the German and the English experience is one of degree. Only two of the twenty-two members of Sabais's original squadron survived. Between 1939 and 1945 the English were, one likes to think, put out to die with a little more care than was exercised by either side on the eastern front. And it was evil things which the English were fighting against. But afterwards? One must agree with Sabais.

This is the context within which Mead's own poetry has to be read. It is a context that theoretically should have been present to any English writer of his generation, but it is one that the majority of his contemporaries either could not, or did not wish to, examine; as far as poetry in England was concerned the war became a European affair. It may have indirectly enflamed the poetic imagination (as in the work of some of the Apocalyptics), and the ordinariness of its hum-drum welfare-state aftermath on this side of the Channel may have contributed to the temperate diction of the Movement poets – but it did not call into question everything that had gone before, its enormities did not paralyse the imagination so that when that stunned faculty did finally re-emerge from its state of shock it was with the hermetic, halting voice of a Pilinszky or a Różewicz. The fact that Mead has lived in West Germany for most of the post-war period, and is a distinguished translator of contemporary German verse, has clearly had a decisive effect on the manner and subject of his own poetry. The opening of the first poem of *Identities*, his first volume of poetry, published in 1967 when the poet was already in his forties, reads like a litany by someone who has barely begun to work free of the war's darkness (and, as the first reference indicates, not only the 1939–45 war's); it is a list of names – Passchendaele, Katyn, Auschwitz, Kronstadt – followed by the phrase 'we stand here'; and then

> What footfall?
> What valley what field what forest
> What streets in the morning sun
> After the streets of Nagasaki?
> Mask, persona,
> Alias, pseudonym,
> We stand here.

The violent and incomprehensible events of the immediate past are beyond the pale of all but the simplest rhetoric, and they appear to reduce the individual and his voice to pathetic insignificance. The repeated 'we stand here' is a statement of incredulity, relief and guilt, but the present seems merely the shell of reality, its mask or alias, compared with what has gone before; it looks backwards for its terms of reference, it is an 'aftermath', haunted by 'something which will, perhaps, never be done with'.

No other modern English poet has quite this tone, though the one who comes closest to it is another poet who knows German literature well, Michael Hamburger. Hamburger and Mead share a liking for sequences of poems, a form that juxtaposes different aspects of reality but seems tacitly to admit that these aspects cannot add up to a single, comprehensible experience; that they belong and do not belong together, that the larger reality they invoke is elusive and unstateable. (I would guess that both poets began by imitating this technique from T. S. Eliot's work, and particularly from *The Waste Land*, a poem which like many of Mead's and Hamburger's presents us with juxtaposed fragments that are to stand for a social whole, vignettes which together evoke the nature of a society whose contradictions seem all but schizophrenic. James Fenton's *German Requiem* is another such poem, and Fenton can occasionally, not only in this poem, sound quite like Mead.)

The second poem of the sequence *Identities* is a love poem; again the subject is one that is defined in terms of the past;

> Will you remember me Tatania
> When your map of this country is folded,
> When you see no more the low tower and the hills,
> The humped bridge, the stream through the osier-holt?
>
>   . . .
>
> Will you remember me Tatania
> As I cling to these landmarks and scars
> Which fade from your mind?

The word 'scars' indicates what is perhaps the fundamental apprehension in Mead's poetry (it is a word which reappears throughout this edition of his collected verse) – that our present existence is marked ineradicably by the past, that it hides a wound from which it can never wholly recover, and that the new tissue, 'the details of moneymaking and manufacture . . . the cocktails and canapés of the social round', is only a tenuous film over this mutilation of our lives and of the body politic. And the juxtaposition of the political brutalities of *Identities'* first poem with the private poignancies of its second poem is typical of Mead's technique and concerns: the obliterating vastness of public ruin is set against the private griefs and celebrations of a love affair – the affair is dwarfed by such a comparison and social débacle is suddenly humanized; it is people who felt such private griefs and hopes – millions of them – who are the statistics of Passchendaele, Katyn, Auschwitz, Kronstadt. The two realities seem barely compatible, and it is their incompatibility that is the horrifying point. Mead refers to

Sabais's liking for Williams's dictum 'No ideas but in things'; his own position can perhaps be better paraphrased as 'No ideas but in facts'; the facts of mass death and private love are set down next to each other as if the poet is saying to the reader 'and what can your mind do with *this*?' 'Nothing' must be our answer, as the poet knows, and his simple statement of the 'facts', his avoidance of all but the most laconic and despairing authorial comment, indicates this.

But Mead's and Sabais's generation did have one great political hope – communism, and specifically Russian communism. To a German adolescent of the 1930s the communists must have seemed the only party that had ever appeared remotely able to stand up to the Nazis, and to an English soldier of the Second World War Stalin could appear as all but an Eastern Messiah. We all know people of this generation who are ready to wax sentimental about Stalin because he fought the Nazis (albeit after trying very hard not to); what he did to his own people in the meantime is dismissed as some kind of unfortunate internal Russian squabble, 'and besides we don't really know what went on'. Sabais, who finally fled from Eastern Germany in 1950, did not of course share this sentimental love for Uncle Joe, and neither does Mead; the destruction of the communist hope haunts his poetry. At the end of his love poem 'To Put a Muse to Sleep' he again juxtaposes the private and public worlds of love and politics to chilling effect:

> the summer night
> narrows, a memory we do not share;
> for as she dreams
> she speaks;
>
> ('Die Russen kommen')

The beloved's dream-murmur refers to the liberation of Eastern Europe in 1945, but the phrase cannot but evoke the cold war and the ways that our own privacies are inevitably hemmed in by politics. His first volume of poems ends with an apparent renunciation of political hope, and the metaphor is typically a military one: 'All who thought they marched to morning / Haunt the watches of the night.' And thirty years on from this moment on Mead was to write what is probably the finest single poem in English on the final extinction of this hope, 'A Sestina at the End of Socialism', a poem which seems almost to choke on its own bitterness, guilt, cynicism, and disillusion:

A dogma ruthless as a rhyme;
The sodding tundra sodden red,
Kulak and gulag, slime and time,
Purge/urge, the duty to be dead.
Ten million roubles bet each way.
The lads are eating horse today.

The word play here is very typical of Mead's technique; the ludic quality of puns, the sensuously beguiling implications of assonance, are used to register anger and impotence rather than pleasure and play; the rhetoric invokes bleakness rather than the light-heartedness and fecundity we usually associate with such devices. The fact that formally the poem is a sestina seems significant. Alongside his free verse Mead has always written poems in tight, strictly metrical, forms, and their proportion vis-à-vis the free verse has increased as his poetry has developed. But in the same way that his tone and subject matter place him to the one side of the preoccupations of his contemporaries, his formal choices also signal a certain distance from what one might think of as the main stream of English verse. He rarely employs the more domesticated imported forms, such as the couplet and the sonnet, which can seem almost wholly English because of their long history within the language, preferring to keep largely to forms that retain much more strongly the aura of their non-English origins, the sestina, the ballade, and with increasing frequency the villanelle.

His poems in such forms, especially those on political events, for example 'Ballade of the Spectre of Communism' and 'Ballade of an Unforeseen Nostalgia', tend to share a tone that is both jaunty, almost ghoulishly so at times, and cynical, and they have something of the colloquial bite of Villon (who via Heine perhaps provided their model); as in Villon's case, we sense a hopeless fury beneath the insouciance. The constant repetitions of the form produce an exasperated 'I told you so' feeling, a sense that we cannot escape from our fundamental insights and premises, that the whirligig of time brings in its revenges by landing us in the same mess we started out from. Many of Mead's poems depend on what can seem to be almost obsessive repetitions for their effect; in the three free-verse sequences that gave him the titles for his first three books of poetry – *Identities*, *The Administration of Things*, *The Midday Muse* – a single phrase is repeated throughout each poem (respectively 'We stand here', 'the dead in mind', 'Name the dead', though the last is confined to one poem in its sequence), and one of his loveliest lyrics, 'And a Merry Meeting', is built on the repetition of a few key phrases. The result can be rather populist, Brechtian even (as in the ballades and sestinas), or it can be that of a mind too shocked to proceed beyond its initial reading of experience (as in the free verse sequences); it can be revivifying and sustaining (as in the lyrics) or it can evoke apathy and ennui, a society unable to lift itself out of hypnotic routine (a tone that is particularly noticeable in his earlier poems). But in each case the device emphasizes the dependence of the present on the past, the ways that experience repeats itself, our knowledge that we cannot escape what we have been. The congruence of formal device with what Mead is actually saying by means of the device is for me one of the most interesting things about his poetry – the form really does embody the message and for once the usually dubious cliché about their being inseparable is true.

Mead is a difficult poet, not because he is particularly obscure (though he is a bit) or allusive, but because he insists on talking obsessively about truths we all want buried because we know, or feel that we know, that we can do nothing about them. To quote his translation of Sabais again, he sets himself against all forms of

> theory-gorged Frenzy,
> which wants simple totality
> instead of difficult truth

against the political utopian whose 'closed image of the world / [is] a penitentiary'. He has had a lifelong involvement with German poetry and certainly his greatest achievement in this field has been his introduction to English speaking readers of Bobrowski – like himself a poet who is in thrall to the past, who is haunted to the point of obsession with what was and is no more – but he has translated many other poets (besides Sabais, Horst Bienek, Günter Bruno Fuchs, Christa Reinig) with equal authority. Though this involvement has set him rather apart from his British contemporaries, as has his insistence on trying to encompass social as well as private realities in his poetry, that is no reason for not reading him (and I do not get the impression that he is read much in England, though I may be wrong); on the contrary his poetry has an integrity and seriousness about it that could only be salutary in effect; and certainly his poetry should be read for itself too, and not merely as an example of a mode alien to most contemporary poets. His tone is unmistakable, and once encountered it is never forgotten; certainly the reader feels sure that Mead's finest poems could have been written by no other poet. Who else could have written this for example (from the beginning of his poem 'Exiles')?

> We dreamed of home as it was and as we were,
> Thronging the known streets with the never-dead
> As if all had not been lost and we were where
> We had always been meant to be; the bay spread
> Before us below the wooded hill, the trees we looked over
> Lopped to preserve the view – to whelm in fire and blood
> And mount again the nightmare of departure.

DICK DAVIS

1984, 2008

Index of Titles